HANDBOOK
OF
PROBLEM
SOLVING

An Analytical Methodology

HANDBOOK
OF
PROBLEM
SOLVING
An Analytical Methodology

Stephen J. Andriole

PBI
a petrocelli
book
new york / princeton

Copyright © 1983 Petrocelli Books, Inc.
All Rights Reserved.

Designed by Diane L. Backes
Typesetting by Backes Graphics

Printed in U.S.A.
1 2 3 4 5 6 7 8 9 10

Library of Congress Cataloging in Publication Data

Andriole, Stephen J.
  Handbook of problem solving.

  Includes bibliographies and index.
  1. Problem solving. 2. Management. 3. Decision-making. I. Title.
HD30.29.A52   1982   658.4'03   82-13345
ISBN 0-89433-186-8

To My Wife Denise Who Continually Amazes and Delights Me

Contents

Preface

ANALYTICAL PROBLEMS of all shapes and sizes surround every analyst, decision-maker, and manager. Yet the methods by which solutions are developed and applied to such problems tend to be static. In fact, analytical problems of all natures are generally approached with routinized and familiar methodologies—regardless of how applicable to the problem at hand they might be. Indeed, methodological myopia is even exacerbated by office proximity, where the location of an analyst's office vis-a-vis his colleague's can determine the number and kind of methodologies considered.

Yet another problem has to do with the time lag connected with the "discovery" and refinement of analytical methods and their introduction into the "field." Too often new methods are conceived and tested in academic or other non-mainstream laboratories and never find their way into the field, or do so only after years have passed. Relatedly, decision-makers seldom have the time or opportunity to learn about new analytical methods on their own and, unfortunately, organizations—be they private or public—infrequently create self-study incentives or offer on-the-job refresher seminars or training courses in analytical methodology.

Finally, there are organizational and situational issues which hover in and around the problem-solving process which are almost always discounted by problem-solvers. Such issues, including problem definition, urgency, and complexity, are generally the most critical to successful problem-solving because they necessarily determine the correct selection and use of competing analytical methodologies. For example, if a problem must be solved in two days by two individuals, how should those individuals select and reject alternative methodologies? Ideally, they would do so based upon situational (in this case, short time and short staff) constraints and related methodological strengths and weaknesses. Unfortunately, however, since relationships among organizational tasks and optimal methodologies are seldom established or explicitly known by decision-makers, unproductive or inappropriate methodologies are frequently selected.

This handbook is targeted at such problems. It is designed to acquaint (and re-acquaint) decision-makers, managers, and analysts with a whole set of methods and techniques which might be of invaluable analytical use to problem-solvers of all kinds. It is explicitly oriented to pragmatic applications; you will find very few purely theoretical discussions here.

The scope of the book is interdisciplinary. Instead of concentrating upon the analytical approaches and methods indigenous to one or two disciplines or fields of inquiry, I have selected for presentation those approaches and methods ripe for application—regardless of their origin. Accordingly, this book is oriented toward bridging the gap between those who develop and test analytical methodology and those who must solve real analytical problems.

The handbook itself is organized around the primary tasks which analysts and managers must perform when they deal with complicated problems. These tasks include:

- ◆ Organization
- ◆ Description
- ◆ Explanation
- ◆ Prediction and Forecasting
- ◆ Prescription (or Decision-Making)
- ◆ Evaluation
- ◆ Documentation
- ◆ "Defense" (Argumentation and Presentation)

Organizational tasks include those which must be performed in order to prepare for successful subsequent analysis. Not unlike the weekend golfer who avoids the practice tee all week, most analysts fail to bring to their analytical problems the set-up skills necessary for successful analysis. Some of these skills include requirements analysis, problem structuring, data identification, and talent, or expertise, assessment.

Requirements analysis and problem structuring involve answering a simple—but too often ignored—question: "What specific kind of analytical problem must I solve?" A good deal of research indicates that far too many of us fail to solve problems because we fail to define them accurately and, consequently, frequently select the wrong problem-solving method.

Problems must therefore be identified, defined, and structured according to their analytical category, substantive nature, urgency, and formality: "Is this a short-range forecasting problem?" "Is it an option selection problem?" "Am I only to describe the situation?" "Have I hours to solve the problem or weeks?" "Will my 'answer' become a report to my boss or will it be primarily for my benefit?" These questions are some of those connected with the organization and problem-structuring tasks.

Data and expertise requirements must also be established before an analysis is undertaken. "Will large amounts of data and an equally strong set of experts be required?" "Can I get the data I need?" "Can a one-man team handle the problem?" "Or will we need a team of experts to generate and process the data?"

Already we can see interrelationships developing: the nature and urgency of a particular problem will determine to a large extent data and expertise requirements. Yet how often are such organizational tasks performed as though they are distinct and unrelated?

Not only do the answers to some organizational questions determine the answers to others, but they all determine the optimal analytical method to be selected. Problem complexity, data requirements, available time, and the like all determine the method best suited to solving the problem at hand.

Descriptive tasks comprise one kind of analytical problem. They are perhaps the most numerous. They can also be the most frustrating and time consuming. But descriptive methods and techniques are also numerous, if not always widely known. They include statistical profiling, taxonomy building, and sampling, among others. On the substantive side, one can select a whole host of approaches to direct and inform such descriptive methods, including historical approaches, psychological approaches, communications approaches, and engineering approaches.

Explanation generally implies and often assumes causality. But causal methodology is not the only methodology by which explanations of events or conditions are generated. While historically skirts are known to rise and fall as the stock market rises and falls, few would suggest any causal relationship between skirt lengths and stock market activity. But many would argue that an *association* exists between the two phenomena. While certainly not as precise as causal explanations, explanations based upon observed associations can constitute useful (though sometimes dangerous) explanations of important phenomena.

Prediction and *forecasting* are often necessary analytical activities. However, few problem-solvers are aware of the many easy-to-use methods at their disposal, methods which range all the way from subjective Bayesian to the hardest quantitative-empirical. These and other methods, as well as the costs and benefits of each, are presented in special detail and context in the handbook.

Often following a descriptive, explanatory, or predictive analysis, decisions must be made regarding which option to implement. This task is *prescription*, and, as with all of the other tasks, there are many available methods ranging from operations research to decision analytic methods and techniques based upon classic (and not so classic) decision tree structuring. A variety of strategies are presented here.

Evaluation problems come in all shapes and sizes. Often problem-solvers are required to evaluate the performance of some piece of equipment, software, reports, people, and options in terms of how they all contribute to a goal or compare against members of the group under evaluation. Most popular evaluation techniques, however, fail to recognize evaluative criteria, criteria weights, and procedures for calculating "worth" logically. Building upon utility theory, the handbook presents several techniques which permit manual or computer-based evaluations.

A special kind of evaluation is *resource allocation* with its associated cost/benefit analytical requirements. The handbook explains those methods based upon subjective criteria and data as well as those which are quantitative-empirical.

All of these techniques require the problem-solver to engage in some form of *modeling* prior to analysis. The handbook looks at models from a functional point of view and discusses the applied essence and proper use of several kinds of models and modeling.

Unless solutions are *documented* properly, they are invariably misunderstood, misapplied, or forgotten. The handbook presents strategies for "packaging" solutions of all natures so that they can be assimilated readily into the administrative and analytical processes of the surrounding environment. These strategies begin with the fundamentals of report preparation and proceed all the way to effective distribution.

Finally, unless a problem-solver can successfully *defend* his or her conclusions, the fruits of labor are generally lost. But how many problem-solvers appreciate or understand the mechanics of solid presentation and argumentation? The handbook examines and illustrates the costs of poor argumentation and presentation and outlines techniques for effective defense.

In addition to all of the above, special attention is given to the *role of the macro-, mini-, and microcomputer in the problem-solving process.* Perhaps surprisingly, in spite of the revolution in analytical and scientific computing, very few problem-solvers are aware of the opportunities and capabilities resident in today's computer—many of which are desktop, inexpensive, and preprogrammed. Computer-based systems for virtually every analytical problem now exist in one form or another and are discussed in detail in problem-solving contexts throughout the handbook. Attention is also given to how a computer-based solution to a recurring or particularly recalcitrant problem or set of problems can be developed cheaply and quickly. Finally, the inappropriateness of some computer-based problem-solving is discussed.

It is hoped that the twelve chapters in this handbook combine to:

♦ Characterize problem-solving as a process comprised of interrelated and interdependent sub-processes.

♦ Increase awareness of antecedent problem-solving requirements and constraints.

♦ Introduce problem-solvers to the array of approaches and methods available for organizational, descriptive, explanatory, predictive, prescriptive, and evaluative problem-solving.

♦ Present techniques for the successful documentation of solutions.

♦ Present techniques for effective solution defense.

♦ Define the optimal role of the computer in the problem-solving process.

Every attempt is made to present the material in a manner consistent with productive use. However, since each chapter might well fill an entire volume, this handbook should not be viewed as a comprehensive text in applied analytical methodology. Bibliographic essays thus appear after every chapter for the reader who wants additional information. Illustrative examples of analytical methodology at work also appear throughout this handbook, and a glossary is presented at the end of the book for quick reference purposes.

Acknowledgments

TEN YEARS ago I began to approach problem-solving systematically. Since then I have studied, misunderstood, applied, and forgotten a lot of analytical methodology. I have also incurred a large intellectual debt along the way to a great many individuals, including—but certainly not limited to—Drs. Jonathan Wilkenfeld, Clinton W. Kelly, III, Don C. Piper, Robert A. Young, and Gerald W. Hopple. Wilkenfeld showed me how to quantify everything. Kelly introduced me to the joys of expert-generated data and the Reverend Thomas Bayes. Piper helped me keep it all in perspective, while Young instructed me convincingly that it is better to solve a problem partially or even temporarily than to debate endlessly about how to proceed. Hopple has witnessed it all and is still improving my work.

I would also like to acknowledge the advice and suggestions of the Central Intelligence Agency's Information Science Center's Office of Training and Education which critiqued an earlier version of this handbook, and Mr. Wayne Norby, of the above office, for the opportunity to present the material to a group of intelligent and forthright professionals.

In spite of this collective debt, I alone am responsible for any errors in the handbook. It is hoped they are few in number and of little real importance.

S.J.A.
Marshall, Virginia

The Process of Problem-Solving

IN SPITE of philosophical arguments to the contrary, all problems are categorizable and solvable. This of course is not to argue that all solutions are durable or that anyone can solve complicated problems. Rather, it is to suggest that problems can be categorized and "solved" *if* one has an appreciation for the general and specific processes of problem-solving *and* an understanding of precisely how the many available analytical methodologies can be most profitably applied.

But what kinds of problems do we most frequently face? Clearly they who generate problems seldom characterize them as belonging to a particular class; nor do they as a matter of course suggest useful analytical methodologies. Instead, problem-generators simply communicate their desire to determine a range of alternative marketing strategies, assess the likelihood of a product price increase, evaluate personnel, and describe in perfect detail "where the money went"; and then they tell you when they need the answer. So long as the answer is clear and relevant to the original problem, the consumer usually cares little about exactly how it was produced. Problem-solvers are thus frequently in a position to select analytical methodologies and thereby exert a powerful influence upon the problem-solving process. Indeed, as we will see elsewhere in this handbook, the selection of a particular methodology can dramatically affect the timeliness, content, and use of analytical solutions; those who select and implement methodologies can therefore dramatically affect the processes of organizational problem-solving in ways which are at times incalculable.

GENERAL PROBLEM-SOLVING PROCESSES

The American College Dictionary defines a *process* as "a systematic series of actions directed to some end." Presumably the series of actions has a beginning, a middle, and an end, and that the actions therein are somehow interrelated.

The notion of process is by no means new. We are all familiar with the processes of government, policy processes, and the processes of internal combustion engines. Yet when we think about analytical problem-solving we tend to see it as comprised of a set of unrelated tasks. Obviously, problems have origins, give rise to analytical strategies, are studied, and sometimes solved. But each of these components is generally treated as relatively independent.

The problem with such perceptions is that they frequently exclude key components of the problem-solving process and, just as dangerously, fail to recognize the dependencies which exist within and throughout the process.

In virtually every professional environment today, problems and the process of problem-solving are characterized by as many "social," administrative, bureaucratic, and organizational variables as they are by substantive analytical ones. No longer is a problem just a problem. Problem-solvers must assess all of their capabilities, organize, analyze, present, and defend their work in a multifaceted environment which may actually inadvertently inhibit the process of problem-solving and the absorption of "findings." For example, as criminal attorneys have known all too well for some time now, the success or failure of one's arguments may depend as much upon the way they are presented as upon how well constructed (that is, how internally consistent) they may be. Similarly, regardless of how competent a problem-solver may be, his or her success or failure may well depend upon the depth and attitudes of available support personnel. Finally, unless the real problem is defined and matched perfectly with the "right" methods and approaches, all is lost.

Graphically, the general problem-solving process can be visualized as suggested in Figure 1.1. Note that regardless of the purposeful nature of the problem-solving

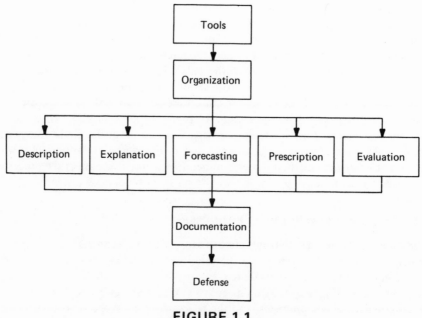

FIGURE 1.1
THE PROBLEM-SOLVING PROCESS

process there are four constants: the assessment of problem-solving tools, organizational tasks, and solution documentation and defense.

SPECIFIC PROBLEM-SOLVING PROCESSES

Figure 1.1 suggests the general sequential steps one should take in order to solve complicated problems but sheds little light upon how one should proceed to solve specific problems. The following chapters survey this terrain. Following discussions regarding the tools of problem-solving and organization, this handbook turns to the specific steps necessary to implement a whole host of computer-based and noncomputer-based analytical methodologies, how to document analytical results, and how to defend the results under conditions of relative organizational harmony and skepticism. Figure 1.1 may thus be treated as the blueprint for this handbook.

SUMMARY

Above all, it is essential that problem-solvers regard problem-solving as a process comprised of a set of interrelated analytical steps which always involve an assessment of tools, the performance of organizational tasks, problem categorization, and solution documentation and defense. Any deviation from this perception will undermine problem-solving efforts.

BIBLIOGRAPHIC ESSAY

Problem-solving is as much a matter of perspective as anything else. For example, one's orientation to change can determine whether or not a problem is resolved. Russell L. Ackoff, in his *The Art of Problem Solving* (New York: John Wiley, 1978) discusses problem-solving flexibility particularly as it applies to problem definition. He also looks at the role which creativity should play in the problem-solving process. The book is also filled with a number of case studies and ends nicely with a chapter devoted to how to keep problems solved. L. Thomas King's *Problem Solving in a Project Environment* (New York: John Wiley, 1981) is also a very useful problem-solving introduction and overview, as are Joseph E. Robertshaw, Stephen J. Mecca, and Mark N. Rerick's *Problem Solving: A Systems Approach* (Princeton, N.J.: Petrocelli Books, 1978), and Charles Magerison's *Managerial Problem Solving* (New York: McGraw-Hill, 1974). In his "Don't Jump to Conclusions," Warren Eberspacher (*Inc.*, August 1980, pp. 67–70) presents a general method for approaching managerial and organizational problems which is grounded in assumptions about the value of brainstorming and group problem-solving. The short article is useful because it presumes that problem-solving is generally too complicated to be attempted by individuals and is most productive when approached by a well coordinated team. Alex Osborn's *Your Creative Power* (New York: Charles Scribner's Sons, 1949) also presents some techniques for group problem-solving and idea generation. Kenneth J. Albert's *Handbook of Business Problem Solving* (New York: McGraw-Hill, 1980) is an excellent compendium of articles on virtually every aspect of managerial and administrative problem-solving with specific sections devoted to management strategy, planning, and control, management organization, staffing, and development, marketing, new product problems, human resources problems, information systems and data processing problems, cost control and cost reduction, production, and physical distribution and materials management problems. While some of the contributions to this enormous volume are targeted at specific substantive problems, many others are generic and therefore of particular relevance to the general process of problem-solving. Similarly, James Adams' *Conceptual Blockbusting* (San Francisco: San Francisco Book Co., 1976), presents some very useful general ideas regarding how to reduce the barriers to accurate problem perception and the flexible conceptualization of solutions.

On a more technical level is Donald F. Mulvihill's edited *Guide to the Quantitative Age* (New York: Holt, Rinehart and Winston, 1966), which attempts successfully to introduce a number of quantitative problem-solving concepts. Herbert A. Simon's *The New Science of Management Decision* (New York: Harper and Row, 1960) is still excellent. His first chapter, "The Executive as Decision Maker," is especially relevant. The first chapter of Hubert M. Blalock, Jr.'s *An Introduction to Social Research* (Englewood Cliffs, N.J.: Prentice-Hall, 1970) is also very relevant because it addresses the complexity of quantitative problem-solving. Two philosophical classics include Israel Scheffler's *The Anatomy of Inquiry* (Indianapolis: Bobbs-Merrill, 1963), and Abraham Kaplan's *The Conduct of Inquiry* (Scranton, PA: Chandler Publishing, 1964). Both are excellent but complicated. It can also be useful to examine the processes of unconventional problem-solving and creative thinking. Osborn's *Your Creative Power* is again relevant. Arthur Koestler's *The Art of Creation* (New York: Dell, 1973); Edward deBono's *Lateral Thinking* (New York: Harper and Row, 1973) and *New Think* (New York: Basic Books, 1967); Sidney J. Parnes and Harold F. Harding's edited *A Source Book for Creative Thinking* (New York: Charles Scribner's Sons, 1962); and Irving A. Taylor's edited *Perspectives in Creativity* (Chicago: Aldine, 1975) also present interesting and useful looks at the processes by which we creatively think, solve problems, make decisions, and manage information, organizations, and people. Eugene Raudsepp's "Nurturing Managerial Creativity" (*Administrative Management,* October 1980, pp. 32–3, 55–6, 75) is targeted directly at individuals within organizations and organizations comprised of inflexible individuals. Several suggestions for "nurturing" creative problem-solving are presented as are some insights regarding the sources of managerial creativity. Finally, John Dewey's *How We Think* (New York: D.C. Heath, 1910) is still one of the best presentations available regarding how we cognitively process information and solve problems.

The Tools of Problem-Solving

INTERESTINGLY, WHEN we have to repair a faucet, tighten a screw, work with wood, or tune-up a car, we carefully select (or purchase) the necessary tools, pick a convenient time, and then go to work. Rationally, if we do not have the necessary tools (and the cost of purchasing new or used ones is prohibitively high), experience, or time to complete the task successfully, we call an "expert" in to help. If we cannot find a competent expert, or cannot afford one, then the work goes undone.

This behavior is interesting because it is logical and routine. Yet when we look at our behavior connected with the execution of analytical tasks which arise in our professional environments, all too often we routinely find ourselves acting illogically by frequently failing to assess our most basic problem-solving capabilities. Instead, we make a series of (often unwarranted) positive assumptions about the tools available to us.

Part of the problem can be traced to the assumptions prevalent in most professional environments, assumptions which often define the very "scope and method" of organizational behavior. For example, while the U.S. federal government's Office of Personnel Management requires the revision of job descriptions almost as frequently as jobs are vacated, job descriptions seldom contain information about what the job-holder is actually supposed to do. Consequently, federal bureaucrats are simultaneously presumed omnipotent and incompetent; omnipotent because job descriptions are (intentionally) vague and sweeping, and incompetent because it is generally impossible to deduce from the job description the precise duties of the job-holder. This vagueness contributes to rising expectations about the position and, secondarily, the position-holder. In practice, one seldom hears federal workers openly admitting that they simply cannot perform a given task. Indeed, if they are experienced they will find a way to deflect or ignore the task; if they are naive, they will attack the impossible task and fail.

Similarly, job descriptions seldom include caveats about expected performance, that is, statements designed to protect a job-holder from the unreasonable or impossible; instead, the formal and informal assumption is that a job-holder should simply do his or her job—whatever it takes.

Finally, the overall professional incentive system by and large punishes the overly careful, organized, and systematic worker and rewards the "can-do" attitude. (How many times have we agreed in our superior's office to perform a task and then back in our own office wondered how we were going to deliver?)

All of this suggests that many of the assumptions and expectations which abound in the professional environment are unwarranted at even the most fundamental levels, and in order to succeed as professional problem-solvers we must understand and appreciate our individual and organizational capabilities. In short, we must at all times maintain an *inventory of problem solving tools*. Specifically, these tools should include:

- ◆ Talent
- ◆ Data and Information
- ◆ Methods
- ◆ Approaches
- ◆ Time
- ◆ Support

TALENT

The relevant questions about talent include:

- ◆ Who?
- ◆ What?
- ◆ Where?
- ◆ How Good?
- ◆ How Much?
- ◆ How to Use?

Questions regarding "Who?" generally apply first to one's self. In other words, a problem-solver must at all times be completely aware of his or her own strengths and weaknesses. If one is thoroughly skilled and experienced with the application of several methods and techniques, then he or she should acknowledge that perhaps the strongest talent can be found seated behind one's own desk. On the other hand, if one's skills and experience are limited, then efforts must be made to identify and use talented in-house and outside associates. Ideally, one's internal environment will satisfy most all problem-solving requirements; however, such is not always the case. Perhaps too often outside associates are necessary, presenting yet another set of problems. Far too frequently outside associates (consultants and the like) may appear ready, willing, and able to perform specific tasks. Unfortunately, while some experts have mastered a great many problem-solving techniques, there are just as many who have only a superficial knowledge of and limited experience with systematic problem-solving methodologies. Accordingly, every effort must be made to identify and select only those outside associates who can meaningfully contribute to the solving of an analytical problem.

It is important to identify specifically those areas of specialization with which the problem-solver is familiar. Just as importantly, assessments must be made regarding the specific strengths and weaknesses of credible outside associates. The areas proposed in this handbook might well be useful for such identification and assessment, recognizing that some individuals are good organizers, describers, and explainers, but relatively poor predictors and prescribers. Similarly, it may be that in-house personnel excel at the tasks connected with evaluation but are relatively weak in the application of computers to the process of problem-solving.

Yet another primary consideration regarding talent has to do with availability. Frequently, talented individuals in just the right areas of specialization are known to us but unavailable. Realistic problem-solving requires that talented individuals be identified, categorized, and made available for problem-solving.

An extremely difficult question concerns assessments regarding the overall quality of certain individuals. "How good" someone is depends to a large extent upon his or her *training, skill, real problem-solving experience,* and *attitude.* While formal academic training is often very useful in the process of problem-solving, it does not unto itself qualify an individual as talented. Indeed there are many holders of advanced degrees who have long since stopped reading and studying.

One's skill in the application of specific methods and techniques may be a better indicator of how useful he or she might be as a member of a problem-solving team. Skillful problem-solvers may or may not have formal training but frequently have a good deal of real problem-solving experience, the next important criterion. Unlike some academically trained individuals, those that possess real problem-solving experience tend to be less preoccupied with the development of theory or the pursuit of truth for its own sake; to the contrary, they tend to be excited about the prospect of actually solving a specific problem.

Regardless of how well trained, skillful, or experienced a problem-solver may be, if his or her attitude is disruptive, overly independent, and/or condescending, among other failings, then he or she is probably not likely to be effective. In fact, it is difficult to underestimate the importance of this criterion. Too frequently individuals with extensive formal training and long resumes are selected to participate in the problem-solving process with little or no regard for the personality undescribed in his or her supporting materials. One problem-solver with the wrong attitude can easily inhibit, misdirect, misinform, and otherwise undermine the entire problem-solving process.

Another important question concerns the optimal use of one's self and in-house and outside associates. Some individuals play their best parts as supporting characters, while others are natural leaders. Very great care should thus be taken with the selection of principal investigators, team leaders, associates, and subordinates.

Figure 2.1 presents a concept regarding the identification and selection of problem-solving personnel. Known as *talent rostering*, the concept suggests that managers, decision-makers, and problem-solvers of all kinds maintain a list of individuals particularly suited to specific problem-solving areas. In the example below a roster appears for the forecasting area of specialization. When completed, as hypothetically suggested in Figure 2.1, such a roster, which should be compiled for all areas of specialization, will enable a problem-solver to identify quickly those in-house and outside individuals best able to solve specific problems as they arise. In addition to this rather simple form, additional information could be maintained on particular problem-solvers, and in a thoroughly modern environment would be accessible via computer terminals.

The idea of a computer-based talent roster is by no means as unusual or unnecessarily luxurious as it might sound. Imagine how much time and effort could be saved if one could generate a list of prospective problem-solvers simply by typing a few words into a computer terminal. The relatively inexpensive computerization process might very well pay for itself in no time at all, especially if installed in an especially active problem-solving environment. Indeed, most conventional data base management systems could easily accommodate the development and use of a talent rostering system for any number of analytical areas. The care and feeding of such a system would, after initial development, really be quite minimal, requiring updating only to add or delete the names of candidate problem-solvers.

The steps necessary to assess, select, and assign talent are as follows:

♦ Who?

Self
In-house problem-solvers
Outside problem-solvers

♦ What?

Areas of specialization

♦ Where?

Availability

AREA OF SPECIALIZATION: Forecasting

Problem-solver	Quality	Cost

FIGURE 2.1
FORECASTING TALENT ROSTER

♦ How Good?

Training
Skill
Real problem-solving experience
Attitude

♦ How Much?

$$$
Other

♦ How to Use?

Task assignment

All of these questions should be answered before any attempt is made to implement an analytical methodology. If inaccurate talent judgments are made, then the whole problem-solving process can be adversely affected. Conversely, if talent judgments are made accurately, perhaps with the aid of a computerized talent rostering system, the process can be accelerated.

DATA AND INFORMATION

All problem-solving must be informed by reliable and accessible data or information. Data comes in many forms but nearly all of it can be categorized according to its epistemological origins. Accordingly, there is hard, or empirical, data, and soft, or "expert," data. We are all familiar with soft data. In its unstructured form, soft data is the essence of experience. Organized according to a set of specific criteria, soft data can take the form of quantitative judgments or opinions. Hard data, on the other hand, is generally derived from the objective observation of selected phenomena in a way which assures reproducibility, verifiability, and validation. A trivial example might concern the level of rainfall during a particular storm: soft data might result from a polling of meteorologists, while hard data might be generated via a rain gauge.

A popular misconception regarding soft data is that it cannot or should not be quantitative or manipulated scientifically. In truth, soft data may be as quantitative as hard data and just as susceptible to scientific analysis.

Another misconception concerns the viability of soft versus hard data. Many problem-solvers believe that the construction of soft data banks is somehow anathema to real problem-solving. In practice, however, soft data banks comprised of, for example, judgments about the likelihood of nuclear war during the next ten years, are often at least as useful as more empirical projections. It is thus very difficult to assess the value of hard and soft data. Instead, one should only attempt to do so within the context of particular problem-solving requirements. For example, when hard data is unavailable, unreliable, or too expensive, available soft data, if relevant, reliable, and affordable, can frequently be used to solve complicated problems. There are also occasions when soft data should be preferred to hard data and vice versa. As a general rule, when a problem is distinguishable by its judgmental characteristics or when virtually no hard precedent data exists, soft data should be preferred. But when a problem is by definition empirical and a great deal of precedent data exists, hard data should be preferred. An example of the first type of problem is a hostage negotiation, while statistical sales forecasting is an example of the second.

Another important consideration regarding the use of (hard and soft) data is its location. For example, frequently a problem may be solved via a less desirable data set primarily because it is available in-house. If time is of the essence, it may be impractical either to acquire or generate data from the outside.

Still another consideration is the reliability of the data or information which is to be used to solve a particular problem. Unreliable data, it is believed, can only yield unreliable results. Similarly, reliable data is expected to yield reliable solutions. Both views are false. "Unreliable" data can in fact yield useful results if the aspects of the unreliability are known prior to its use, and "reliable" data in the wrong hands can produce disastrous solutions.

It is important to remember that all data is to some extent unreliable. Data utility is a function not of precise measures of reliability but rather familiarity; when a problem-solver is very familiar with a particular data set or data base it is likely to be used productively, but when a data set is unfamiliar to a problem-solver it is much more likely to be misused.

One of the most important aspects of data and information is its format. If reliable and available hard or soft data is scattered throughout a hundred reports and memoranda it can be of no use to a serious problem-solver; on the other hand, if relatively "unreliable" available hard or soft data is neatly arranged or (ideally) computerized, then it will probably find its way into the problem-solving process. Also, whenever data is collected or acquired anew, it should be formatted in a way which will yield maximum future use. Organizations and individual problem-solvers should all *standardize* the collection, acquisition, and storage of information which might be used to solve future problems.

Surrounding all of these data characteristics is cost. Generally it is extremely expensive to collect or acquire new data. It can be even more expensive to reformat existing data. But such costs are not experienced simply in dollars. Time, lost opportunities, and lost support are all legitimate data costs.

Finally, it is important to remember that *massive* amounts of information and data already exist in many and varied forms from hundreds of independent sources, sources which by and large go unused by most problem-solvers (who prefer to go without or create new and often redundant data sets). Some of these data sets are accessible from on-line computer banks. Two of the most notable are the *New York Times* Information Bank and Lockheed's Dialog system.

The *New York Times* Information Bank provides an on-line and an on-demand information service. Updated daily, it contains a data base of abstracts of news stories, essays, surveys and other material published in the *New York Times* and over 70 other newspapers and periodicals, including the *Wall Street Journal, Business Week,* the *Washington Post*, and the *Los Angeles Times.* Approximately 20,000 new abstracts are added monthly. The data base is current from 1969. The system itself is designed to respond to the information requirements of corporations and managers, libraries and librarians, and government agencies and officials.

Figure 2.2 illustrates one piece of information extracted from the *New York Times* Information Bank. The figure shows the 14th item of a total of 46 items retrieved. The microfiche number enables the terminal operator to obtain a microfilm copy of the full text of the article. The publication in which the article appeared appears next, followed by the date of the publication. The "PHO/ILS" entry indicates that a photographic illustration accompanied the article. The column and page number are next, and the remaining items in the heading are the system accounting entries.

Lockheed's Dialog Information Retrieval System is another system which collects, stores, organizes, and permits access to an enormous data base. In his excellent "Information Unlimited: The Dialog Information Retrieval Service" (*Byte*, June 1981, pp. 88–108), Stan Miastkowski lists the most popular Dialog data bases. They include:

- ◆ ERIC (Educational Resources Information Center), which contains information on training and education.

- ◆ ABI/INFORM, which contains abstracts from administrative, organizational, and management publications.

- ◆ SSIE Current Research, compiled by the Smithsonian Science Information Exchange, which contains abstracts of on-going and recently completed U.S. government-funded research projects.

- ◆ Magazine Index, which contains an index of over 350 U.S. magazines (since 1976).

- ◆ GPO Monthly Catalog, which presents the monthly catalog of U.S. Government Printing Office publications.

- ◆ Conference Papers Index, which contains an index to scientific and technical meetings, conferences, and symposia as well as references to the papers presented at these meetings; approximately 10,000 new citations are added each year.

- ◆ DISCLOSURE, which contains extracts of Securities and Exchange Commission (SEC) filed reports by all publicly owned U.S. corporations.

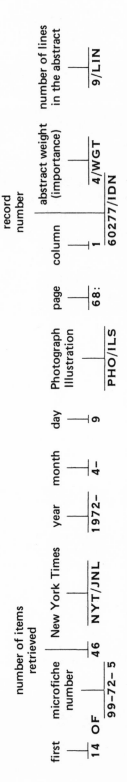

number of items retrieved

record number

first	microfiche number	New York Times	year	month	day	Photograph Illustration	page	column	abstract weight (importance)	number of lines in the abstract
14 OF	99-72- 5	46 NYT/JNL	1972-	4-	9	PHO/ILS	68:	1	4/WGT	9/LIN
								60277/IDN		

ARTICLE ON GROWING POPULARITY OF ROTARY ENGINE CARS IN US; WANKEL ROTARY ENGINE IS MAJOR MODIFICATION OF INTERNAL COMBUSTION ENGINE; DELIVERS SAME HP AS INTERNAL COMBUSTION ENGINE TWICE ITS SIZE BUT THERE IS LESS WEAR BECAUSE ROTARY ENGINE ELIMINATES NEED FOR PISTONS AND HAS ABOUT 40X FEWER MOVING PARTS; WAS 1ST INTRODUCED IN US IN '70 AND 2,098 CARS WERE SOLD THAT YR; MAZDA MOTORS, WHICH MFRS RX-2 ROTARY ENGINE CAR PREDICTS '72 US SALES COULD REACH 60,000; ILLUS COMPARES STANDARD 6-CYLINDER ENGINE WITH MAZDA ROTARY ENGINE

FIGURE 2.2
NEW YORK TIMES INFORMATION BANK SAMPLE OUTPUT

♦ Encyclopedia of Associations, which contains a listing and detailed information on approximately 15,000 U.S. nonprofit organizations, including professional societies, trade associations, cultural and religious organizations, and labor unions.

♦ Standard and Poor's News which contains information and financial reports on over 9,000 companies.

♦ NTIS, compiled by the National Technical Information Service of the U.S. Department of Commerce, which contains citations to over 700,000 U.S. government and government-sponsored research and development reports.

In addition to these information sources are literally thousands of scientific and technical library and reference facilities throughout the country. The American Society for Information Science maintains a list of such facilities. Similarly, the Information Industry Association (IIA) maintains a list of all public and private information sources. IIA's list is enormous and can direct a problem-solver to most any kind of information. If all else fails, the Defense Documentation Center (DDC) can be the source of endless numbers of reports, as can virtually all national and international government offices and agencies, especially the United Nations and World Bank.

Finally, two of the best locators of information are the *Inventory of Information Resources and Services Available to the U.S. House of Representatives* compiled by the U.S. House of Representatives Commission on Information and Facilities, and the University of Michigan's Inter-University Consortium for Political and Social Research (ICPSR).

All of the above information sources, which are by no means comprehensive, suggest that incalculable amounts of information are constantly being compiled and disseminated. Before a problem-solver begins to analyze a problem, some time should be spent canvassing existing data sets.

Internally, problem-solvers should maintain lists of their own, as suggested in Figure 2.3. Such inventories will prevent problem-solvers from creating or acquiring data they may already have and suggest data which ought to be acquired for future use.

The potpourri of government and foundation research reports available directly from the sponsoring organization or through the computer-based information systems is a particularly valuable problem-solving tool. Without question there will be times when the problem at hand has already been solved or at least defined. It is on such occasions when a little time and money can be very well spent.

Finally, it should be pointed out that this handbook draws no important distinction between data and information. Unlike too many organizational and managerial theorists and practitioners who believe that data is unfocused information, data and information are interchangeably treated here.

TYPE		LOCATION		RELIABILITY		FORMAT		COST	
Hard	Soft	In	Out	High	Low	Good	Bad	High	Low

FIGURE 2.3
DATA INVENTORY

In summary, the relevant questions concerning data and information are as follows:

- ♦ What?

    Hard (empirical)
    Soft ("expert")

- ♦ Where?

    In-house
    Outside

- ♦ Reliability?

- ♦ Format?

- ♦ Cost?

    $$$
    Time
    Other

METHODS

The identification, selection, and use of an appropriate method usually poses a much more difficult and controversial problem to the problem-solver. Initially, before one can settle upon a comfortable and appropriate method, one should settle the attending epistemological issues. In short, this amounts to a stating if only to one's self the particular epistemological bases from which the problem is to be attacked. The basic distinction, of course, lies somewhere between the rationalist and empiricist epistemological orientations. Methodologically, this distinction translates into the basic distinction between quantitative and qualitative methods, which may be broadly conceived and regarded as mutually exclusive, but in practice by no means incompatible.

Problem-solvers employing qualitative methods are likely to rely primarily upon their own personal and individual qualities, that is, upon their wisdom, intuition, experience, values, and judgments.

Quantitative methods refer to all those involving measurement of any kind. Moreover, those employing quantitative methods are generally very concerned about precisely how the measurement is handled. The result of these (and other) preoccupations has lead to an emulative stage where some problem-solvers have attempted to be as scientific as possible. In the social and behavioral sciences, for example, this stage has sired a methodology which may be regarded as a direct offshoot of the social and behavioral scientific desire to emulate the methodology of the natural or physical sciences.

After the physical sciences, then, the social sciences have attempted to develop their own methodology, quantitative in nature and definitely procedural in design.

Thus, the popular "scientific method" with its composite and logical steps has been embraced and, in certain circles, even reified. Succinctly, the goals of the social and behavioral scientific method include the searching for regularities or patterns which are assumed *a priori* to exist; the development of testable hypotheses and propositions; the production of verifiable and replicable generalizations; and, ultimately, the construction and application of empirically verified theories.

Ancillary to the fundamentally quantitative and qualitative methods are a number of other problem-solving methods which are autonomous to the extent that they may be employed regardless of the particular epistemological orientation of the user. There are, thus, inductive, deductive, and comparative problem-solving methods. Briefly, induction involves the production of knowledge through the observation and examination of what is considered to be the real, or universal, environment. Knowledge is produced when the observer's experiences check with "reality". Deduction, on the other hand, refers to the production of the knowledge which is extracted directly from one or more analytical premises. Knowledge is thus produced when experience checks with the premises and not necessarily with reality.

No attempt is made here to declare one methodological orientation superior to the other. In practice, it is the problem-solving situation which should determine the selection of an analytical method. For example, when the U.S. intelligence community wants to know when and where a nuclear war might break out, it relies upon qualitative methods and expert-generated data, but when it needs an estimate of Soviet grain production, it gathers and analyzes a great deal of empirical data about Soviet weather, soil conditions, equipment, and agricultural expertise.

Methods may thus be classified according to some rather broad criteria, as suggested below:

♦ Qualitative

Inductive
Deductive
Comparative

♦ Quantitative

Inductive
Deductive
Comparative

APPROACHES

The terms *approach, method,* and *technique,* are all too often employed interchangeably. *Approach,* by far, is the most frequently employed; problem-solvers of all kinds constantly refer to, for example, sociological approaches, legalistic approaches, and even quantitative approaches.

An approach consists of criteria for selecting the questions and data to address a problem. Approaches can be categorized according to two rather broad criteria: affinity to already existing academic disciplines, and affinity to particular functional features of the phenomenon or problem under investigation.

Approaches identified with academic disciplines are hardly strange to many problem-solvers. Indeed, there are *at least* as many approaches to problem-solving as there are social, behavioral, and physical science disciplines. Obviously all problem-solvers from time to time employ a historical approach. Problem-solvers who desire to concentrate upon concepts as diverse as culture, society, roles, organizational behavior, and the like are often said to have adopted a sociological approach. These problem-solvers generally focus upon the sociological subject matter which impinges and exerts an influence upon the particular problem in question. In addition to historical and sociological approaches are economic, psychological and geographical approaches, just to name a few. As in the case of all of the approaches identified with academic disciplines, problem-solvers adopting a particular approach borrow directly from the disciplines.

In addition to approaches identified with academic disciplines are those which emphasize, or dwell upon, a particular feature or aspect of the phenomenon or behavior in question. Some of these approaches include the institutional approach, the legal approach, the structural approach, the systemic approach, and the communications approach.

Approaches can thus be classified according to how they relate to each other conceptually, as suggested below:

♦ "Disciplined" Approaches

Historical
Sociological
Economic
Psychological
Geographical . . .

♦ Functional Approaches

Institutional
Legal
Structural
Systems
Communications . . .

TIME

In the words of Merrill E. Douglass and Donna N. Douglass, two well known time managers, time is an illusive sunbeam, an evaporating raindrop, a wilted dandelion on a windy day. Indeed, there is no question that the availability and use of time is of critical importance to the overall problem-solving process. Ironically, however, this important aspect of problem-solving is almost completely ignored by most problem-solvers. At the most specific level, problem-solvers should be cognizant of the amount of time available and necessary to solve a particular problem; but at the more general level, problem-solvers should be aware that their problem-solving effectiveness is to a great extent determined by how well or badly they manage all of their time.

As many time managers point out, most problem-solvers labor under a whole set of misconceptions about the management of time. Many believe, for example, that no matter how well organized one is there is never enough time to accomplish all that needs to be done. Many believe that time is a constant in the problem-solving equation; still others are convinced that they are efficient time managers of at least their own time. In reality, of course, the modern office environment massproduces opportunities for wasting time. The so-called drop-in visitor, who arrives just when you are trying to concentrate on a complicated problem, is a perennial time waster. Unnecessary and unnecessarily long telephone conversations are other common problems as are inefficient meetings, poor verbal and written communications, ill-planned local and out-of-town travel, and personal and staff disorganization. It is important to recognize the real frequency and impact of these time wasters, however, and fully understand just how much our organizational, administrative, and bureaucratic environments breed time-wasting opportunities. Today, so very much of our time is spent either on the telephone or around a conference table. Increasingly, we find ourselves arguing about procedural details and waiting forever for the myriad signatures necessary to gain approval to do anything. Some have referred to such problems as inherent to the "bureaucratization of the world," but here it is safe to regard them as serious obstacles to problem-solving.

Those who try to make problem-solvers more effective through the improved management of time generally propose the elimination or reduction of time-wasteful activity coupled with the systematic allocation of available time resources. Clearly the elimination or reduction of wasteful activity is the key to the efficient utilization of time. In other words, the best way to systematically allocate time resources is to increase such resources, especially since many problem-solvers do not have schedules predictable or routinized enough to always permit rigid time planning.

One's general approach to time management should extend to the management of problem-solving time. Like talent, data, methods, and approaches, time is a tool that must be used properly. Most importantly, it should be used to determine what can and cannot be attempted in a problem-solving situation. One should also remember that too much time can be as detrimental to successful problem-solving as too little time. The availability of too much time can induce procrastination and methodological overkill, while too little time can jeopardize the application of even the most straightforward analytical methodology.

In summary, the following guidelines can help with the efficient management of time:

- ◆ AccurateTime-Use Perceptions

  Time as a limited resource
  Time as a manageable resource

- ◆ Control of Time-Wasting Activities

  Drop-in visitors
  Unnecessary telephone conversations
  Unnecessarily long telephone conversations
  Inefficient meetings
  Poor verbal and written communications
  Ill-planned local and out-of-town travel
  Personal and staff disorganization

- ◆ Time-Use Planning

  Time scheduling
  Time monitoring

SUPPORT

Talented problem-solvers with access to necessary data and in full command of methods, approaches, and time, will usually fail unless adequate support exists. The overall importance of support is analogous to the computer science notion of throughput, or the processes by which information, decisions, and solutions are formulated and flow through their organizational surroundings.

The most important component of support is people. Here the reference is to typing and production support, research support, and administrative or procedural support. Fast, accurate, and reliable people are absolutely necessary for successful problem-solving.

Information is another kind of support. Ideally, necessary problem-solving information may be acquired in-house; if not, effective means for the creation or acquisition of outside data must be established. If internal procedures are unsupportive or nonsupportive, then problem-solvers will find themselves inhibited by administrative fact and fantasy. Accordingly, serious problem-solvers ought not lose sight of the potential impact of administrative and bureaucratic policies and procedures upon the problem-solving process. If procedures are found to be unsupportive or nonsupportive, then the problem-solver should petition to have them changed. For example, if a particular problem requires the use of an outside data base which is neither free nor immediately available, and internal procedures forbid (because of lack of funds) the purchase of outside data, then problem-generators should either refrain from posing such problems or arrange for funds to cover data acquisition contingencies. The key here is the identification and communication of support limitations. Similarly, if typing and research support is unavailable to solve a particular problem, and there are no in-house means to alleviate the shortage, then problem-solvers by their own communicated acknowledgment should not be held responsible for generating solutions.

Yet another component of support is the number, nature, and quality of available machines. On the mundane side, perhaps, are the typewriters and reproduction machines available for problem-solving use; and on the more sophisticated side are computerized word processors and other computerized routines useful for effective data storage, manipulation, and analysis. If a secretary has to travel several floors to copy a piece of paper, or retype a page five times without the aid of a memory typewriter, then it is safe to say that the problem-solving process will probably not be consistently competitive. Interestingly, many experienced problem-solvers will attend to all of the tools necessary for successful problem resolution except those which comprise the overall tools of support. Without *all* of the necessary tools, the process of problem-solving will be undermined.

The components of support are summarized as follows:

- People

  Typing and production
  Research
  Administration

- Information

- Procedures

- Machines

  Typing and reproduction
  Computers

SUMMARY

The intriguing aspect of the role of problem-solving tools is that its importance is so frequently discounted by experienced managers, decision-makers, and planners. For example, while great effort may be expended to assemble just the right mix of problem-solving expertise, hardly any will be spent to determine whether or not the experts will be well supported. In fact, when compiling research budgets planners will sometimes deliberately reduce the number of proposed support hours to make room for more and more technical personnel. Of course technical personnel cannot function without adequate mechanical, logistical, and human support. All problem-solving plans should thus include realistic estimates about the nature, quality, availability, and cost of support. Those on the receiving end of such plans should also be aware of realistic expertise/support ratios. Similarly, very few problem-solvers actively support efforts to build up-to-date internal reference and professional libraries—until a critical need arises. Too many methods and approaches go unapplied simply because they are unfamiliar, and too many "experts" are selected on the basis of considerations other than skill, experience, cost, and availability.

It is impossible to overestimate the importance of the tools of problem-solving. All successful applications of analytical methodology depend upon their proper use and all unsuccessful applications can be traced to their improper use. Throughout this handbook the importance of these tools will be highlighted. Note how every single applied methodology is dependent upon the skillful use of the tools of problem-solving.

BIBLIOGRAPHIC ESSAY

The literature on problem-solving talent and expertise is diverse and broad, and infrequently focused directly at the assessment and application of expertise in analytical problem-solving contexts. Nevertheless, numerous relevant articles can be found in sections 2 and 5 of Kenneth J. Albert's edited *Handbook of Business Problem Solving* (New York: McGraw-Hill, 1980). Similarly, Leon A. Wortman's very recent *Effective Management for Engineers & Scientists* (New York: John Wiley, 1981), while primarily aimed at "high technology" project management, is a very useful presentation of "people problems" and the means to deal with them. Specifically, Wortman looks at the needs and motivations of organizational problem-solvers, ways to build productive interpersonal relationships, cope with negative and abrasive personalities, build team activity, how to use management styles effectively, and how to solve twelve common people-management problems. Wilbert W. Scheer's *Personnel Administration Handbook* (Chicago: Dartnell, 1981) is a good source book, as is James J. Cribben's *Effective Managerial Leadership* (New York: American Management Association, 1972). Josh Martin's "Taking the Risk Out of Choosing and Using Consultants" (*Computer Decisions*, April 1981, pp. 58–71) is a specific guide to the selection and use of outside help. Oriented explicitly to choosing and using computer consultants, it is extremely useful to anyone in need of a consultant. Martin deals extensively with when, who, and how to hire, stressing experience and consultant management. He also deals with what to expect from consultants and what to pay for their services. Eugene Raudsepp's "Delegate Your Way to Success" (*Computer Decisions*, March 1981, pp. 157–8, 163–4) is a short but very focused article about how to best use available talent via skillful delegation. Of special value is Raudsepp's questionnaire for determining whether or not you are delegating enough. Finally, William S. Hubbartt's "The Delicate Art of Firing" (*Administrative Management*, April 1981, pp. 22–3, 42–4) is a valuable article to have available when things turn sour with a permanent employee or consultant. Hubbartt not only looks at the procedures which enable one to dismiss an employee in the most straightforward way possible, but he also pays special attention to what can and cannot be done under existing Federal equal employment opportunity laws.

D.M. Brownstone and G. Carruth's *Where to Find Business Information* (New York: John Wiley, 1979) is one of the best compendia of available data and information. The large volume contains information about newsletters, magazines, reference texts, and computerized data bases. It is also well indexed. Matthew Lesko's "Get your Facts Straight from Washington" (*Inc.*, August 1980, pp. 38–41) is of course much more focused, but almost as valuable as the Brownstone-Carruth volume because Lesko helps you penetrate the Federal bureaucracy. For example, he points out correctly that enormous amounts of information about foreign cultures and foreign investment opportunities are available directly from the Central Intelligence Agency and the U.S. International Trade Commission. It is also possible to obtain information from the Congressional Research Service, the Congressional Information Service, the U.S. General Accounting Office, the U.S. Federal Trade Commission, the Justice Department, and the U.S. Department of State, among countless other research firms, offices, and agencies which collect and maintain information of all kinds. Lesko also provides a directory of Federal information sources complete with 88 phone numbers. But be forewarned: Lesko reports that an average of seven telephone calls is necessary to zero in on a generally illusive information target. Another source of Federal information is the large aforementioned *Inventory of Information Resources and Services Available to the U.S. House of Representatives*, compiled by the U.S. House of Representatives Commission on Information and Facilities and published by the U.S. Government Printing Office (Washington, D.C., 1976) and the Greenwood Press (Westport, CN, 1977). But in addition to the information available from Federal offices and agencies, this volume also contains a listing of some private information resources. Of more general interest are the volumes which list and describe all of the available reference texts, such as Alden Todd's *Finding Facts Fast: How to Find Out What You Want and Need to Know* (Berkeley, CA: Ten Speed Press, 1979), and Marion V. Bell and Eleanor A. Swidan's *Reference Books: A Brief Guide* (Baltimore: Enoch Pratt Free Library, 1979). These two short volumes can save you a lot of time and trouble because they index the myriad general reference texts on the market today and even suggest how to track down information not immediately available.

The key to all of this is first a familiarity with general sources of information (almanacs, yearbooks, reference texts, computerized retrieval systems, and the like) and, second, a constant search for new and unusual material via an aggressive and never-ending canvassing of information updates, directories, publications lists, and computer-assisted searches. Realistically, however, unless one has access to a full-time staff, the sheer volume of new information will bury the average problem-solver. Consequently, it is essential that problem-solvers with repetitive outside information needs become thoroughly familiar with his or her area(s) of specific responsibility. Such "sub-set information management" is possible and usually cost-effective. For example, while it might be impractical or impossible to maintain a comprehensive library of foreign policy materials, it would be possible to compile and monitor information pertinent to U.S.-Japanese trade policy as it pertains to automobile imports to the U.S.

The literature on analytical methods and approaches can be found within the covers of more general titles. For example, Israel Scheffler's *The Anatomy of Inquiry* (Indianapolis: Bobbs-Merrill, 1963) and Abraham Kaplan's *The Conduct of Inquiry* (Scranton, PA: Chandler Publishing, 1964) are once again of interest. Much less philosophical are *The Manager's Guide to Statistics and Quantitative Methods* by Donald W. Kroeber and R. Lawrence LaForge (New York: McGraw-Hill, 1980) and *Quanti-*

tative Analysis Methods for Substantive Analysts by Henry F. DeFrancesco (Los Angeles: Melville Publishing, 1975). Some behavioral science treatises on methodology can be found in Hubert M. and Ann B. Blalock's *Methodology in Social Research* (New York: McGraw-Hill, 1968) and Fred N. Kerlinger's *Foundations of Behavioral Research* (New York: Holt, Rinehart and Winston, 1973). Finally, Earl R. Babbie's *The Practice of Social Research* (Belmont, CA: Wadsworth, 1975) is extremely readable and valuable to an understanding of the essence of quantitative analysis.

The literature on time management is, perhaps surprisingly, broad and voluminous. Merrill E. and Donna N. Douglass' *Manage Your Time, Manage Your Work, Manage Yourself* (New York: Amacom, 1980); Norman Kobert's *Managing Time* (New York: Boardroom Books, 1980); R. Alec MacKenzie's *New Time Management Methods* (Chicago: Dartnell, 1980); Harold Taylor's *Making Time Work for You* (New York: Beaufort Books, 1979); and Robert D. Rutherford's *Just in Time* (New York: John Wiley, 1981) are all excellent. Much shorter pieces include F.D. Barrett's "Everyman's Guide to Time Management" (*The Business Quarterly*, Spring 1973, pp. 72–8); "Teaching Managers to Do More in Less Time" (*Business Week*, March 3, 1975, pp. 68–9); Eleanor B. and R. Alec MacKenzie's "Time Management for Women" (*Management Review*, September 1977, pp. 19–25); and R. Alec MacKenzie's "Toward a Personalized Time Management Strategy" (*Management Review*, February 1974, pp. 10–15). In addition to these and many other published materials are a number of time management seminars and courses given several times a year in countless cities across the country which attempt to teach the fundamentals of effective time management in a few hours, a day, or a week. While most of the time management literature and training seminars stress time analysis, scheduling, and planning, the real leverage lies in the identification and control of time-wasting activity.

Information about the role of support, as it has been defined here, is scattered. Wayne L. Rhodes' "How to Boost Your Office Productivity" (*Infosystems*, August 1980, pp. 36–42) does, however, blend several notions together in an interesting way. Rhodes suggests, for example, while support personnel and facilities are extremely important to office productivity, it is to the behavior of the decision-maker vis-a-vis support personnel that real boosts in productivity can be traced.

3

Organization

AS IT RELATES to problem-solving, organization is comprised of five distinct sets of activities:

♦ Requirements Analysis

♦ Problem Identification

♦ Problem Structuring

♦ Constraint Analysis

♦ Project Management

REQUIREMENTS ANALYSIS

Requirements analysis is necessary for successful problem-solving simply because it is the basis upon which problems are ultimately structured and solved. Too frequently problems are tackled on the basis of *perceived* requirements only. Consequently, very often excellent solutions are generated which are unrelated to the particular problem at hand, resulting in the well-known solution-in-search-of-a-problem syndrome.

The first step toward the conduct of requirements analysis is the collection of data or information about the pending problem. Some very basic techniques include the use of questionnaires, Delphi surveys, ad hoc working groups, and interviews. Some more sophisticated techniques include critical incident profiling, the conduct of job analyses, the running of simulations, and the development of fault trees. All of these are designed to extract from the problem-generator and solution-consumer precise information about his or her problem.

Questionnaires, Delphi surveys, ad hoc working groups, and interviews are really designed to answer two questions: "What do you do?" and "What do you want?" The questions themselves should be structured generally and specifically, that is, with reference to the general problems which the consumer faces as well as to the specific problem at hand. It is also important to get a feel for how often certain problems occur and for whom the problems within the chain of command are addressed. Finally, it is important to understand *why* certain individuals solve particular problems.

The use of simple questionnaires to obtain information about the consumer's job and specific problem is inexpensive; however, questionnaires sometimes make it difficult to be specific enough to extract detailed information. Delphi surveys, a technique in which the recipient's responses are fed back anonymously, are also relatively inexpensive, and often promote consensus and the identification of information requirements from the participants. Ad hoc working groups can alleviate some of these problems, especially at the very high administrative and/or managerial levels. Straight interviews with problem-solution-consumers to determine information requirements, organizational constraints, and the like are used more or less universally. However, to apply this method successfully the interviewer must be experienced and familiar with structured interviewing techniques (see the section on Surveys in chapter 4).

The essence of these techniques of course lies in their attempt to capture or profile precisely that which it is that a problem-generator requires. Again, information should be sought at the general level (for anticipating future problems and information requirements) and at the specific level (in order to identify the specific problem at hand).

Job analyses, critical incident profiling, and simulations are more complicated. Job analysis techniques, such as task analysis, link analysis, and activity analysis, which attempt to characterize user requirements from direct observation, are probably more applicable to tasks which are managerial and administrative, rather than analytical. In other words, job analysis techniques are much more difficult to apply to cognitive tasks. Critical incident profiling, during which users are asked via interviews or surveys for information about particularly important "incidents" or information requirements, can be extremely useful. Here the intention is to capture the primary problem-solving requirements while ignoring the relatively secondary ones. The use of simulations for the conduct of requirements analyses should be restricted to those cases where the problem-solving environment is particularly complicated and repetitive. "Paper" simulations, during which participants are stimulated by human observers in order to obtain information about the participant's problem-solving and information-seeking behavior, tend to be relatively expensive and time consuming. "Protocol analysis, " during which the prospective problem solution-consumer comments extensively on his or her activities during simulated problem-solving, is even more expensive, obtrusive, and detailed. Finally, interactive computer-based simulation or gaming is very expensive, time consuming, and complicated, and should be used only during those cases when it is impossible to identify problem-solving and information requirements and when a good deal of support and time is available.

Yet another, somewhat different, technique for locating and defining analytical problems involves the development of fault trees. Fault trees can represent the "findings" from more conventional requirements analyses, but they are by no means dependent upon such analyses. In other words, fault trees can be used as alternative-requirements gathering tools.

Fault trees can be used to decompose systems, organizations, and even human relationships in order to pinpoint why they malfunction. For example, Figure 3.1 presents a simple fault tree for diagnosing why a computer system is not used productively. Notice that there are several levels in the tree and that the levels are interrelated.

In order to develop a fault tree like the one in Figure 3.1, one should proceed from the general to the specific. Each general and specific set of possible problems should be arranged hierarchically, and the sets themselves should be mutually exclusive. As organizing devices, fault trees can be used to identify and evaluate specific elements for check-off purposes. Fault trees may thus be used to orchestrate a process of elimination. But they may also be used to conduct more sophisticated trouble-shooting analyses via the assignment and combination of malfunction probabilities. The assignment of probabilities (or likelihoods) to the elements of the fault tree can help pinpoint the problem in an efficient way. By so "pruning" a fault tree (by simply checking each and every element or by assigning probabilities), problem-solvers can trim the tree down to the problem branch which must be "solved."

But the use of fault trees is not without problems. First, unless experts are used to develop the tree it can easily grow too large. Second, it is sometimes difficult to decompose a system or organization into analyzable parts. Because of this, many fault trees have large branches labeled "other problems," and are consequently only of limited value. Finally, problem-solvers should be aware that fault trees are most applicable to problem classes which are to some extent known before tree development begins. Problems which are completely unknown to problem-solvers are probably better located via some other means (which might then enable the problem-solver to develop a fault tree).

All of these techniques are designed to prevent fundamental "disconnects" which constantly arise between the problem-generator and the problem-solver. Such disconnects are especially prevalent in research and development and when problem-generators are primarily administrators and problem-solvers and more analytical in training and function. However, since the conduct of requirements analyses always consumes analytical resources, problem-solvers should guard aganist launching requirements analyses which are disproportionate to the problems they are intended to identify.

The methods available for problem profiling include the conduct and/or development of the following:

- ◆ Questionnaires
- ◆ Delphi Surveys
- ◆ Ad Hoc Working Groups
- ◆ Interviews
- ◆ Formal Job Analyses

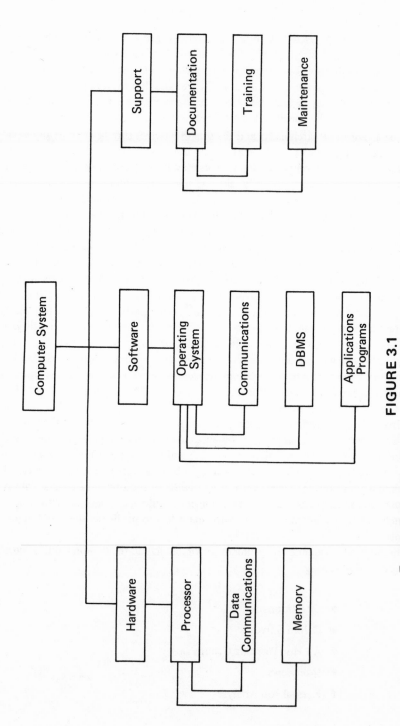

FIGURE 3.1

FAULT TREE FOR COMPUTER SYSTEM PRODUCTIVITY PROBLEM

♦ Critical Incident Profiles

♦ Simulations

♦ Fault Trees

PROBLEM IDENTIFICATION

If requirements analyses are continually and successfully conducted, it is unlikely that there will be any serious problem identification errors. Of critical importance is the categorization of pending problems into one or more meaningful slots. The classificatory scheme used in this handbook is one which recognizes seven distinct kinds of problems. They are:

♦ Description

♦ Explanation

♦ Prediction/Forecasting

♦ Prescription

♦ Evaluation

♦ Documentation

♦ Defense

It is possible to categorize most any problem into one or more of these substantive areas. Of greater importance, however, is the degree of understanding which exists between the problem-generator and problem-solver regarding these categories. In other words, once a problem has been identified or "scoped," closure must be sought regarding the classification.

If necessary, several iterations regarding the pending problem's nature should be encouraged. Indeed, consumer feedback at this point can be extremely valuable. A simple technique regarding such closure is the Problem Certification Memorandum. Briefly, this memorandum can be used to communicate to the consumer the problem-solver's perspective. In addition, the memorandum should require the consumer to agree with the problem-solver's perspective in writing, as suggested in Figure 3.2.

The important considerations here are the following:

1. The classification of a problem into a specific category.

2. A mutual understanding regarding this classification between the problem-generator and the problem-solver.

TO: Problem-Generator

FROM: Problem-Solver

After several meetings, discussions and/or written notices, our office/ group/division/team will proceed on your problem which we regard as consisting of the following:

_____

_____

_____

_____

_____

_____

Please concur by signing below. We will proceed as quickly as possible upon receipt of the signed memorandum.

                                        Problem-Solver

Accepted <u>Problem-Generator</u>

Rejected _____

Date   _____

FIGURE 3.2
PROBLEM CERTIFICATION MEMORANDUM

PROBLEM STRUCTURING

Another organizational step necessary for successful problem-solving involves accurate problem structuring. There are at least three productive problem-structuring techniques which to a greater or lesser extent involve the use of:

- ◆ Analogy
- ◆ Models and Frameworks
- ◆ Hypothesis Formation

Analogy is one of the most powerful problem structuring methods available. It is also one of the easiest and most pragmatic methods to use. How often do problem-solvers sit around a conference table recalling a previous problem while discussing a current one? In practice, it happens all of the time. The suggestion here is to *formalize* the practice to some degree in a manner likely to yield the maximum benefit from previous work.

The suggestion to formalize is grounded in managerial research which indicates that most analytical problem-solving is repetitive. Logic thus suggests that enormous amounts of information can be gained from an examination of these repetitive cases. Accordingly, before a problem is structured for analysis, a set of questions should be answered regarding its similarity to previous problems. On the antecedent side, quick reference lists comprised of previous problems should be maintained. Such lists should recognize various problem types, such as description, explanation, prediction, prescription, and evaluation, and should be consistently compiled so that an "institutional memory" can be established.

Another problem-structuring technique involves the use of models and/or frameworks. A model is a simplified representation of some aspect of reality. Models are simplified because it is impossible to fully represent the entire complexity of a real phenomenon, process, or behavior, regardless of its nature. Models and frameworks can be descriptive, explanatory, predictive, prescriptive, or evaluative. It is thus possible to model how something works, why something works, when something will work, how, why, and when something should work, and how well it works. As abstractions of reality, models are of limited use, but since models and frameworks are created by the problem-solver the limitations are generally known.

All graphic schematics are models as are maps and instructions for the assembly of bicycles and toys. The key to the use of models and frameworks is the comfortable representation of a phenomenon, process, or behavior. If it is overly complex, it will be unusable, and if it is overly simple, it will be useless.

If a problem is descriptive in nature, then a schematic of its nature and scope may be extremely useful. For example, the process of problem-solving may be modeled descriptively, as suggested in Figure 3.3.

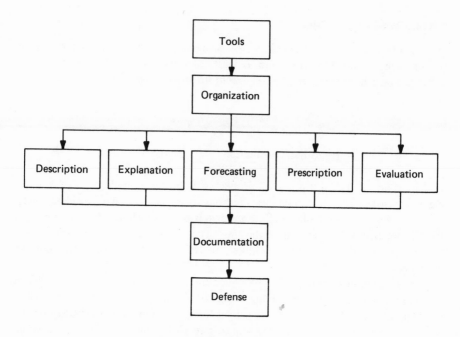

FIGURE 3.3
THE PROBLEM-SOLVING PROCESS

The real value of models and frameworks lies in their controlled simplification, their pinpointing of interrelated parts, and the mapping of the interrelationships among the parts. In a very real sense, then, modeling is akin to dividing and conquering.

Models are also useful in the formation of hypotheses, another useful problem structuring tool. In the scientific literature, a hypothesis is a statement about the relationships among phenomena usually expressed in "if . . . then . . ." form. "If he wins in New York, then he will win the presidency," is an example of a hypothesis. Hypothsis formation is especially useful for structuring explanatory and predictive problems, but can be useful in other kinds of problem-solving as well.

One way to use hypotheses productively is to solicit them from experts and then subject them to the scrutiny of another set of experts. In this way it is possible to identify, evaluate, and then pinpoint the most promising problem hypothesis.

In summary, there are at least three useful problem-structuring techniques which are grounded in analogy, modeling and framework construction, and hypothesis formation.

CONSTRAINT ANALYSIS

After consumers and solvers have agreed upon the nature and substance of a particular problem, problem-solvers should conduct systematic constraint analyses regarding what it is they can reasonably accomplish during the alloted time and given the problem's requirements. There are five kinds of constraints that ought to become the focus of constraint analyses. They are:

- ◆ Time Constraints
- ◆ Manpower Constraints
- ◆ Data Constraints
- ◆ Support Constraints
- ◆ "Bureaucratic" Constraints

Time constraints are perhaps the most straightforward. If an answer is required within the day, there is a clear limit to the amount of problem-solving that is possible. At the other extreme, if months are available to solve a particular problem, then a problem-solver can feel relatively unconstrained. To a great extent, unrealistic expectations and frustrations often evolve from inaccurate time estimates. Accordingly, problem-solvers should be explicitly aware of their own capabilities in relation to available time. One simple method of time estimation involves record-keeping. For example, previous decision-making, forecasting, and evaluation problems ought to be documented with reference to their complexity and expended time. Imperfect and biased memories should not be relied upon to generate accurate time estimates.

Another constraint has to do with available manpower. Even if adequate time is available to solve a problem, without the necessary personnel, time itself becomes an irrelevant variable. A simple device for the conduct of manpower constraint analysis is the use of a talent selector, as suggested in Figure 3.4. The selector, which requires the problem-solver to list associates according to their availability, quality, and cost, will quickly enable one to determine whether or not he or she can assemble a first-rate team. If not, then consumer expectations must be lowered.

Data constraints are as critical as time and manpower ones. Without adequate data, problem-solving results will probably be suspect and narrow. A data selector, as shown in Figure 3.5, can aid a problem-solver with the selection and assessment of useful data.

Support constraints are also of critical importance. If a report is due during the weeks when a problem-solver is especially short-staffed, then in all likelihood he or she will miss perhaps an important deadline. If typewriters and reproduction equipment are in short supply and of poor quality, then again deadlines may be placed in jeopardy.

Problem: _Forecasting_

Preparer: _____

Date: _____

FORECASTING PROBLEM-SOLVER	AVAILABILITY		QUALITY		COST	
	High	Low	High	Low	High	Low

FIGURE 3.4
TALENT SELECTOR

Problem: _____*Forecasting*_____

Preparer: _____

Date: _____

FORECASTING DATA	LOCATION		RELIABILITY		FORMAT		COST	
	In	Out	High	Low	Good	Bad	High	Low

FIGURE 3.5
DATA SELECTOR

TOOLS	AVAILABILITY	
	YES	NO
TALENT		
DATA		
METHODS		
APPROACHES		
TIME		
SUPPORT		

FIGURE 3.6
PROBLEM-SOLVING CHECKLIST

Finally, "bureaucratic" constraints must be assessed. If established administrative /bureaucratic procedures are non-supportive and inhibiting, then the entire project may be undermined.

All of this should reduce to a checklist regarding the availability or non-availability of the key components of the problem-solving process. Such a checklist need not be complicated or timeconsuming and may in fact reduce to a simple mental operation regarding whether or not a particular problem-solving operation is in a "go" or "no go" mode. (A simple problem-solving checklist might resemble the one presented in Figure 3.6.)

PROJECT MANAGEMENT

Following the conduct of requirements analyses, problem identification, problem structuring, and the conduct of constraint analyses, the problem-solver should plan how he or she will manage the problem-solving process. There are at least three excellent project management techniques. They involve the use of:

- ♦ Milestone Charts
- ♦ Gantt Charts
- ♦ CPM Charts

Milestone charts are simple to use and of enormous value before, during, and after a project. Before a project begins, it is always useful to identify the project's expected accomplishments across the period of time during which the project is scheduled to take place, as suggested in Figure 3.7. During a project, a milestone chart facilitates immediate project monitoring, while after the project it permits ex post facto evaluations.

Gantt charts are very similar to milestone charts but display how long each important task should take in addition to completion dates. Gantt charts thus display more information than milestone charts, as Figure 3.8 suggests. They are also superior monitoring and evaluation tools because they permit manager's to track project progress very closely; they also display visually the co-pursuit of project tasks.

Neither milestone nor Gantt charts depict the interrelationships among project tasks. Task dependencies can, however, be displayed nicely in CPM charts. CPM (Critical Path Method) charts, known variously as "network plans," "arrow diagrams," and "PERT diagrams," enable a problem-solver to diagram any sequence of project tasks. They also enable managers to estimate how long each task should take and calculate the effects of delays in task scheduling, all as suggested in Figure 3.9 with reference to the development of an interactive computer software system. Note that in the figure the flow of project activity is represented by left-to-right arrows and each circle (or activity mode) represents the point at which one task ends and the next begins.

The development of a CPM chart is a logical extension of milestone and Gantt chart development, which is not to imply that CPM chart development is excessively time consuming. In fact, milestone, Gantt, and CPM charts are all relatively easy to develop after a problem has been profiled. They should also only be developed after a systematic constraint analysis has been conducted.

The above project-management tools are presented according to an implicit complexity continuum, as summarized below:

♦ Milestone Charts

 Task Schedules

♦ Gantt Charts

 Task Schedules
 Task Time Estimates

♦ CPM Charts

 Task Schedules
 Task Time Estimates
 Task Interrelationships

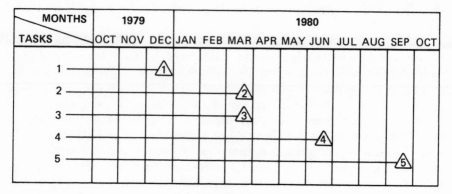

FIGURE 3.7
MILESTONE CHART

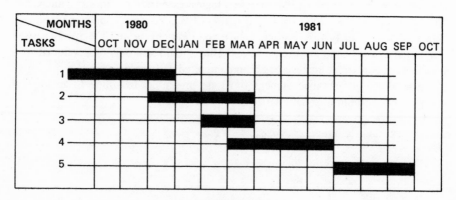

FIGURE 3.8
GANTT CHART

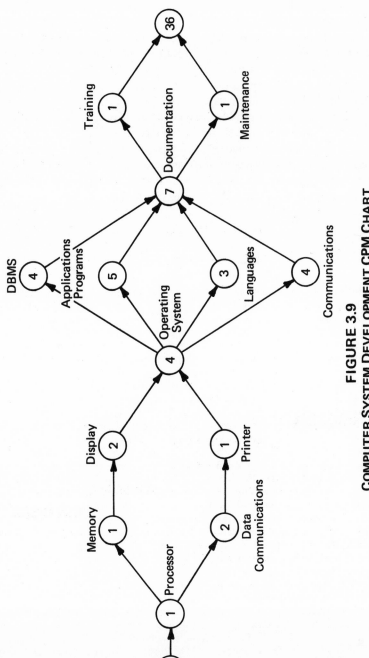

FIGURE 3.9
COMPUTER SYSTEM DEVELOPMENT CPM CHART

SUMMARY

The overall organization task involves the successful completion of many sub-tasks. The conduct of requirements analyses constitutes the initial critical step. Problem identification and problem structuring are equally critical, but dependent upon the results of requirements analyses. Realistic constraint analyses follow all of the above but precede project planning and management.

As with the assessment of problem-solving tools, it is difficult to overestimate the importance of organization tasks and sub-tasks. Yet frequently these are precisely the tasks shortchanged by harried analytical problem-solvers. Admittedly, the tasks which comprise the organization task are some of the least exciting in the entire problem-solving process. But it is also true that a great many project and problem-solving failures can be traced directly to organizational failures.

BIBLIOGRAPHIC ESSAY

The literature on requirements analysis is usually general and can therefore be found with reference to many different requirements problems. For example, an excellent discussion of requirements analysis can be found in H. Rudy Ramsey and Michael E. Atwood's *Human Factors in Computer Systems* (Englewood, CO: Science Applications, September 1979). While oriented to the design and development of interactive computer-based systems, it deals in detail with virtually all available requirements analysis methods. Also of general interest are J.C. Flanagan's "The Critical Incident Technique" (*Psychological Bulletin*, 51, 1954, pp. 327–358); "A Review of Information Requirements Techniques," by W.M. Taggart, Jr. and M.O. Tharp (*Computing Surveys*, 9, 1977, pp. 273–290); and C.A. Bennett's "Toward Empirical, Practicable, Comprehensive Task Taxonomy" (*Human Factors*, 13, 1971, pp. 229–235). For a solid look at interviewing, questionnaire design, and survey methodology, see Earl R. Babbie's *The Practice of Social Research* (Belmont, CA: Wadsworth, 1975) and Delbert Miller's *Handbook of Research Design and Social Measurement* (New York: David McKay, 1970), as well as the Bibliographic Essay in chapter 4 of this handbook. The literature on simulation is vast, but a useful introduction can be found in Richard E. Trueman's *An Introduction to Quantitative Methods for Decision Making*'s (New York: Holt, Rinehart and Winston, 1977) Chapter 14 entitled, "Simulation Models." Requirements analysis via the development of fault trees is illustrated in A. E. Greene and A. J. Bourne's *Reliability Technology* (New York: Wiley-Interscience, 1972) and *Fault Trees: Sensitivity of Estimated Failure Probabilities to Problem Representation* by B. Fischoff, P. Slovic, and S. Lichtenstein (Eugene, OR: Decision Research, August 1977), which also contains a look at the strengths and weaknesses of fault trees.

Perhaps the most fundamental approach to improved problem identification can be gleaned from the literature in cognitive psychology and perception, but a quicker route would include L. Thomas King's *Problem Solving in a Project Environment* (New York: Wiley-Interscience, 1981). Problem structuring research should lead you to Charles A. Lave and James G. March's *An Introduction to Models in the*

Social Sciences (New York: Harper and Row, 1975), Babbie's *Practice of Social Research*, Trueman's *Quantitative Methods for Decision Making*, and the references on statistical methodology which appear in chapters 4, 5, 6, and 7 of this handbook. Nearly all of them contain good discussions of models, frameworks, and hypothesis formation.

The formal literature on constraint analysis usually hides under the name "resource allocation," but rather than spending a lot of time digging through material which will tell you little about how to conduct a very specific constraint analysis, the recommendation here is to proceed directly to the task using a log of previous time, manpower, data, support, and bureaucratic estimates. In other words, your own record-keeping and experience will become your best applied constraint analysis methodology.

Finally, one need look no farther for an excellent project management reference text than Steve Erikson's *Management Tools for Everyone* (Princeton, N.J.: Petrocelli Books, 1981). But if you must look beyond this book, Donald W. Kroeber and R. Lawrence LaForge's *The Manager's Guide to Statistics and Quantitative Methods* (New York: McGraw-Hill, 1980), and Richard E. Trueman's *An Introduction to Quantitative Methods for Decision Making* (New York: Holt, Rinehart and Winston, 1977) both contain excellent discussions of some very useful project management techniques.

4

Description

TYPICALLY, PROBLEM-SOLVERS describe conditions, situations, and problems in narrative form via memoranda, letters, and short reports. This procedure is obviously unstructured and unsystematic, yet can sometimes yield excellent results (especially when time is short and the object of the description is qualitative). However, when time, data, talent, and support are available, a great many simple statistical techniques can be used productively to describe events, conditions, situations, and processes.

UNIVARIATE STATISTICAL PROFILING

Quantitative-empirical and subjectively or expert-generated data, when it represents a single variable, can be used to profile the variable in a number of meaningful ways. First, it should be pointed out that quantitative data can be generated viably via subjective and objective means, as discussed in some detail in chapters 2 and 3. Statistical operations can be performed on both subjective and objective data, and productive analytical use can therefore be made of both kinds of data.

Univariate, or single variable, profiling of sales or population distributions, for example, can be used to present information to superiors or colleagues in and out of specific problem-solving contexts. Such information can be presented in tabular or graphical form; it can also be operated upon.

Univariate Tabular and Graphical Displays

At the basis of all univariate displays is the frequency distribution which, in turn, facilitates the discovery of the average values and overall spread of quantitative data. Figure 4.1 presents a simple frequency distribution in graphical form. The vertical line in the graph is the ordinate and plots the variable frequencies, while the horizontal line is the abscissa and plots the values of the variable. Figure 4.2 presents data in a histogram, also known as a bar graph when time is not a major descriptive object of the display. Finally, Table 4.1 suggests how information can be arranged in tabular form.

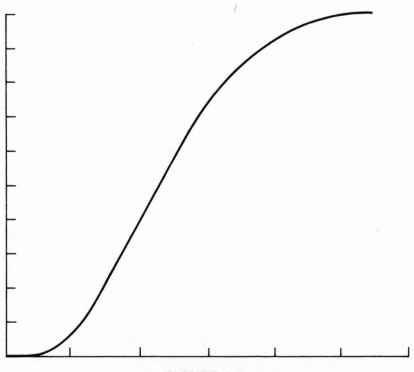

FIGURE 4.1
GRAPHIC FREQUENCY DISTRIBUTION

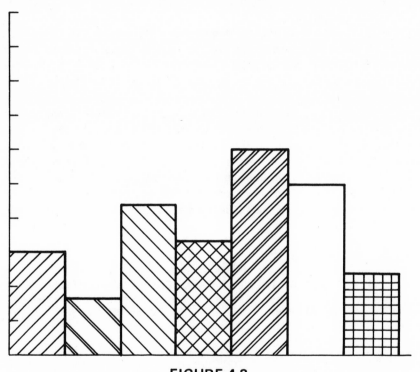

FIGURE 4.2
HISTOGRAM

It is important, however, to recognize that there are different kinds of objective and subjective quantitative data, and that these kinds affect how to present and manipulate data. Information which refers to variables like colors and organizational grades, or a variable which is categorizable in other than measurable ways, is *nominal*. Information which refers to variables like budgets and sizes is *ordinal* when it can be directly measured, and *interval* when it can be measured vis-a-vis an explicit measurement standard.

The construction of a useful frequency distribution thus depends upon the kind of data one is working with. When working with nominal data and variables, one can graph, chart, or tabulate frequencies quite easily. But when working with ordinal data, one should make sure that the order of the variable values and the variable ranges are specified. Interval variables should be plotted or tabulated by specifying the values of the variables, the number of variable intervals, and the sizes of the variable intervals.

Table 4.2 illustrates how a nominal table can be constructed. In the example, the number of available U.S. aircraft in the event of a national or international emergency is listed according to three nominal categories: military, commercial, and privately owned. Figure 4.3 presents this information on a bar chart. Table 4.3 illustrates the construction of an ordinal variable frequency table of sales districts and their respective sales as a percentage of their expected quotas. Figure 4.4 displays the same information. Finally, Table 4.4 and Figure 4.5 present some interval data.

TABLE 4.1
HYPOTHETICAL TABULAR FREQUENCY DISTRIBUTION

Variable	Frequency
1	x
2	x
3	x
4	x
5	x
6	x
7	x
8	x
9	x
10	x

TABLE 4.2
NOMINAL VARIABLE FREQUENCY DISTRIBUTION

Aircraft	Frequency [*]
Military	8,000
Commercial	6,000
Private	4,000

[*] Hypothetical Data

TABLE 4.3
ORDINAL VARIABLE TABULAR FREQUENCY DISTRIBUTION

Sales Districts	Rank	% Quotas
D	1	94%
F	2	87%
I	3	81%
A	4	70%
J	5	66%
H	6	61%
G	7	50%
C	8	47%
E	9	40%
B	10	31%

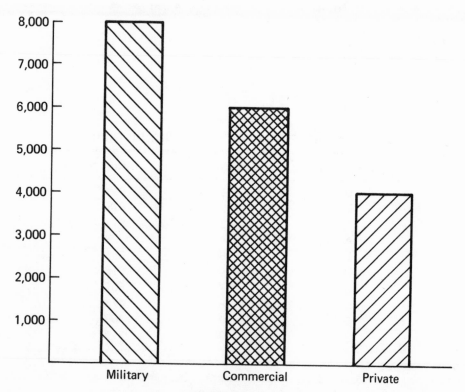

FIGURE 4.3
NOMINAL VARIABLE BAR CHART

TABLE 4.4
INTERVAL VARIABLE TABULAR FREQUENCY DISTRIBUTION

Salesperson Age (Intervals)	Sales (Frequency)
21–25	6
26–30	9
31–35	12
36–40	15
41–45	16
46–50	20
51–55	25
56–60	30
61–65	10

Univariate Statistical Operations

Quantitative data about costs, sales, benefits, and the like can be tabulated, graphed, and plotted, as suggested above. But one can also perform a series of operations which can yield a great deal of insight into the nature and potential use of the data. All of these operations can be classified as measures of central tendency or measures of variability.

Measures of central tendency include the median, mode, and the mean of the variable which is the object of description.

The *median* is the score of the variable which has as many cases above it as below it. It is directly in the middle of the total number of observations. If there are five tellers and the median number of customers they receive is 300 per week, then half of the tellers receive more customers and half receive fewer customers than 300 a week.

The *mode* is the classification with the greatest number of observations. On a corporate board there may be more numbers who are fifty years old than any other age. Fifty is thus the modal age for the board.

The *mean* is the mathematical average, or the result of the total number of observations divided by the number of cases.

Measures of variability include the range and the standard deviation (from the mean).

The *range* measures the highest and lowest values of the data. For example, if the percentage of salespersons that have reached their sales quotas across twenty-nine U.S. states is 96% in the highest (and, in this case, "best") and 14% in the lowest (or "worst"), the range is 14% to 96%.

The *standard deviation* from the mean or average value of the variable under description is useful for determining just how deviant a given value is relative to all of

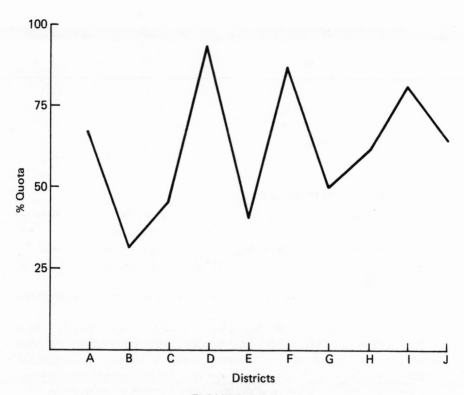

FIGURE 4.4
ORDINAL VARIABLE GRAPHICAL FREQUENCY DISTRIBUTION

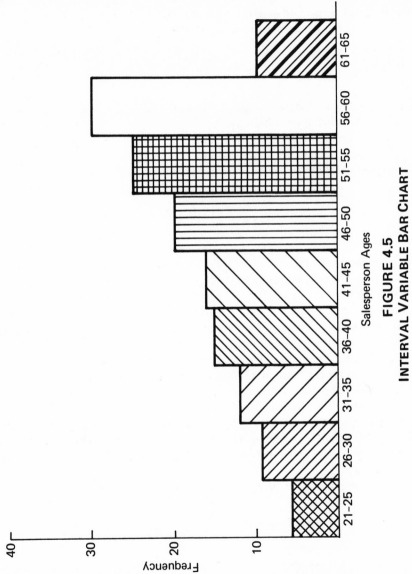

FIGURE 4.5
INTERVAL VARIABLE BAR CHART

the values. For example, how average is a salesperson's sales relative to the whole sales force? When the individual salespersons have fairly similar sales, then the standard deviations for the salespersons will be very small. But when the figures are vastly different, then the standard deviations will be great.

Computing the standard deviation is straightforward, as follows:

$$S = \sqrt{\Sigma X^2 - \bar{X}^2}$$

where S =   standard deviation computed for a sample of data;
      X =   the value of any observation;
      $\bar{X}$ =   the mean of all observations; and
      N =   the total number of observations.

A variation of this formula can be presented as follows:

$$S = \sqrt{\frac{\Sigma X^2}{N} - \left(\frac{\Sigma X}{N}\right)^2}$$

$\frac{\Sigma X^2}{N}$ instructs one to square and total the values of each observation; then divide by the total number of observations. $\left(\frac{\Sigma X}{N}\right)^2$ tells one to add the values of the observations, and square the result. Finally, subtract the second result from the first and then compute the square root of the difference.

All measures of variability facilitate an analysis of the differences which exist within the data which is to constitute some kind of description. Fortunately, a great many computer programs exist which calculate medians, modes, means, ranges, and standard deviations in a flash, so it is now possible to generate and compare all kinds of calculations and graphic and tabular displays in a matter of minutes.

The profiling of single variables can significantly improve the process of problem-solving by injecting rigor and precision into the descriptive process. Specifically, statistical profiling enables problem-solvers to replace guesses and rough approximations with very explicit frequency distributions, measures of central tendency, and measures of variability.

In summary, then, univariate profiles can be presented and computed as follows:

◆ Data Displays

    Tables
    Graphs
    Bar charts
    Histograms

◆ Data Operations

Measures of central tendency

Median
Mode
Mean

Measures of variability

Range
Standard deviation

BIVARIATE STATISTICAL PROFILING

Bivariate, or two variable, profiles describe the relationship between two variables, like the rate of crime and the rate of unemployment. As with univariate profiling, one can graphically display bivariate relationships and perform various statistical operations upon bivariate data.

Bivariate Tabular and Graphical Displays

Three bivariate displays include contingency tables, rank-orders, and scatter plots.

Contingency tables are used primarily with nominal or ordinal data. For example, consider a descriptive problem involving the relationship between sales levels and the age of salespersons. Sales levels, for the purpose of this example, can be defined simply as high and low, while age can be defined as under forty years of age and over forty years of age. Now assume a hypothesis that states that the older the salesperson the higher the sales. Table 4.5 presents a contingency table for this hypothetical relationship and suggests quite clearly that salespersons over forty years of age have higher sales levels than salespersons under forty.

Contingency tables can be used to describe all kinds of relationships when the data is available and when the descriptive problem is well formed. They can also be used in multivariate situations, that is, when more than two variables comprise a descriptive hypothesis (see chapter 5).

Rank-order displays can also be used effectively to describe relationships among variables. Especially appropriate for ordinal data, rank-order displays can help describe bivariate interrelationships via a simple criss-crossing technique which enables problem-solvers to locate relationships visually. Figure 4.6, for example, presents the salespersons, this time by name, according to their sales figures and age. The criss-crossed rank-order diagram makes it very easy to see (once again!) that the older salespersons are more successful than their younger counterparts.

TABLE 4.5
SALESPERSON/SALES CONTINGENCY TABLE

Sales		Salesperson Age: Over 40	Salesperson Age: Under 40	
	High	100	16	116
	Low	32	148	180
		132	164	296

Scatter plots, or *scatter diagrams,* also facilitate the visual inspection of ordinal or interval bivariate data. The salespersons' age and sales example once again (Figure 4.7) illustrates how a graphical display can enhance the description and understanding of univariate, bivariate, and multivariate data. Finally, Figure 4.8 illustrates how a *coordinate graph* can display positive and negative values for two variables. As can be seen, the coordinate graph focuses attention upon data groups which might not otherwise be evident in tabular or other graphical form.

Bivariate Statistical Operations

All of the above techniques for the description of bivariate data and relationships tell nothing about the degree of the relationships. The amount of bivariate covariance can be measured by a number of operations which can yield a precise description of the degree to which the variables vary with one another.

For nominal data, *Yule's Q* can be used to measure the degree of association between two variables. It also yields information about the direction (positive or negative) of the relationship.

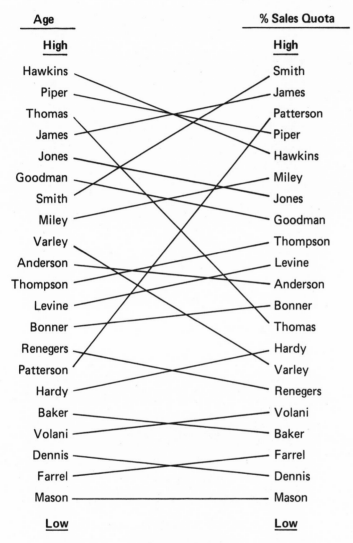

FIGURE 4.6
SALESPERSON/SALES RANK-ORDER DISPLAY

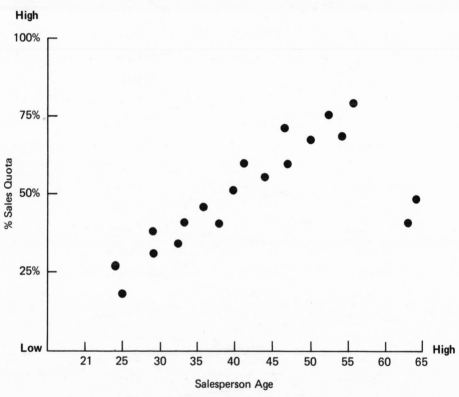

FIGURE 4.7
SALESPERSON/SALES SCATTER PLOT

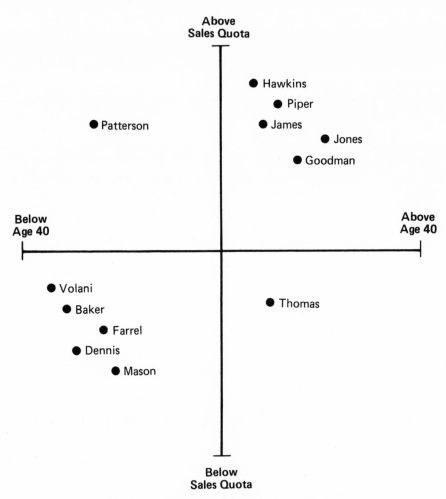

FIGURE 4.8
SALESPERSON/SALES COORDINATE GRAPH

Yule's Q can be computed only on a two-by-two table, such as appears in Table 4.5 above. Table 4.6 suggests how Yule's Q can be computed, and Table 4.7 presents the results of a Yule's Q calculation on the hypothetical sales data.

Yule's Q is useful because it can be used on raw numeric variables or on variables in percentage form. At the same time, whenever a zero appears in any one of the four cells in the two-by-two table, Yule's Q will always come out "perfectly" (that is, ±1.0).

Another nominal data statistic is the *Chi Square* test, which checks the probability that the differences between observed and expected variable frequencies are random. (Observed frequencies are those for which we have actual data, while expected frequencies are those deduced from hypotheses, expert judgments, and/or prior experience.) Table 4.8 illustrates the computation of Chi Square, or X^2. Note that unlike in the computation of Yule's Q, the computation of Chi Square involves the use of the two-by-two marginals.

The Chi Square test will inform one just how likely the "null hypothesis" (that the two variables are unrelated) is, but in order to use the test properly one must deal with the statistical notion of "degrees of freedom." Degrees of freedom determine the flexibility one has to change the entries in a contingency table and still remain statistically significant, that is, well within the range of non-randomness. X^2 must thus be checked against values for statistical significance against specific degrees

TABLE 4.6
COMPUTATION OF YULE'S Q

x

a	b
c	d

y

$$\text{Yule's } Q = \frac{ad - bc}{ad + bc}$$

of freedom, which vary according to the number of cells in the contingency table (more information on degrees of freedom and statistical significance can be found in chapter 5 and in the many sources cited in this and the next chapter's Bibliograpic Essays).

Ordinal level statistical operations include Spearman's rho, which, like Yule's Q, measures the degree and direction of an association ranging from -1.0 to +1.0, while an interval level association test includes the computation of the product moment correlation coefficient, which measures the strength of the relationship between the variables. The product moment correlation coefficient does not, however, indicate a causal relationship between two variables, nor does it measure a correlation, in the explanatory sense, of two variables. (Correlation will be discussed in chapter 5.)

The use of contingency tables, rank-order displays, and scatter plots, as well as the statistical operations which accompany them, facilitates the description of bi-variate, or two variable, relationships in ways which permit problem-solvers to display, measure, and chart relationships quantitatively and comparatively. Like uni-

TABLE 4.7
SALESPERSON/SALES YULE'S Q CALCULATION

Salesperson Age

	Over 40	Under 40	
High	a 100	b 16	116
Low	c 32	d 148	180
	132	164	296

$$\text{Yule's } Q = \frac{100 \times 148 - 16 \times 32}{100 \times 148 + 16 \times 32} = .93$$

TABLE 4.8
CHI SQUARE CALCULATION

x

a	b	e
c	d	f

y

g   h   N

$$\text{Chi Square } (X^2) = \frac{N(ad - bc)^2}{(a + c)(b + d)(a + b)(c + d)}$$

variate displays and statistical operations, bivariate displays and operations can all be generated and executed easily with computer support. However, considerable *applied* expertise is necessary to implement all statistical procedures, expertise which can be expensive and sometimes difficult to find. Data requirements are also substantial when even simple statistical operations are performed. Finally, with computer support, univariate, bivariate, and (especially) multivariate statistical operations should require relatively little time; however, without computer support the same operations can deplete even the largest time reserves.

The bivariate displays and operations discussed above can be summarized as follows:

♦ Data Displays

Contingency tables
Rank-orders
Scatter plots

♦ Data Operations

Yule's Q
Chi square
Spearman's rho
Product moment correlation coefficients

SURVEYS

Survey research constitutes a general-purpose approach to many varied descriptive problems. Surveys can be used to define problem-solving requirements, poll experts about likely production problems in the 1990s, and gather information about attitudes, beliefs, and behavior. But they are difficult to conduct properly.

Survey data can be generated by conducting interviews or by mailing out so-called self-administered questionnaires. It is critical that the survey questions be diagnostic of the descriptive problem at hand; hence, questionnaire design lies at the heart of any useful survey. Similarly, if the survey is to be conducted via interviews, then adequate training must be given to the interviewers.

In order to conduct a representative sample, that is, one which measures what it is supposed to measure, it is necessary either to sample every member of the sample population or sample a limited but representative sub-sample. Since it is infrequently possible to sample an entire population, problem-solvers should become familiar with sampling techniques (see the Bibliographic Essay below). An example of how biased sampling can occur includes the 1936 *Literary Digest* presidential poll which predicted that challenger Landon would receive 60% of the vote and defeat President Roosevelt. Landon received only 38% of the vote. A retrospective analysis revealed that middle and high income subscription lists had been used to collect the survey data. One must therefore be especially careful to sample in a manner which will ensure that the data will be representative of the target population.

All surveys require a good deal of expertise in quesionnaire design, sampling, interviewing, and administration. Mailed questionnaires are generally less expensive than those administered directly because interviewers do not have to be trained or hired. On the other hand, interviewers are usually more successful at getting responses than are mailed questionnaires, which more often than not fail to return or return incomplete. Obviously, then, mailouts require a great deal of time and support.

In summary, the critical elements of surveying inlcude:

♦ Interviews and Mailouts

Questionnaire design
Representative sampling
Survey administration

CLASSIFICATORY SCHEMA, TAXONOMIES, AND TYPOLOGIES

Classificatory schema constitute one of the simplest and most powerful descriptive tools available to problem-solvers. Very succinctly, classificatory schema are narrative lists of events, conditions, processes, or entities which classify phenomena on the basis of similarities and differences. In practice, classificatory schema are often used as organizing devices for the collection of data and the visual identification of hypothetical relationships. The key to the development of useful classificatory schema lies in the development of meaningful comparative categories and the consistent application of the categories.

Taxonomies are similar to classificatory schema, although in the minds of some analysts taxonomies are somewhat more formal than classificatory schema. Both classification techniques require the development of comparative categories and both are systematic.

Typologies, on the other hand, are generally perceived as much more formal, precise, and powerful than classificatory schema or taxonomies. At the same time, typologies are much more difficult to develop than classificatory schema or taxonomies. The typological procedure requires that every member of the population be classified in only one of the major classificatory categories. This requires the typological terms to be mutually exclusive. Accepted typological construction requires that typologies predict all aspects of its type. For example, from type 1 in a given typology it would be possible to predict the existence of a number of specific characteristics with great accuracy. Classificatory schema and taxonomies are usually much less precise than typologies.

SUMMARY

All of these descriptive techniques and methods can be used to "solve" all kinds of descriptive problems. Recalling that enormous amounts of data exist (and is continually being collected), the basic statistical techniques discussed can lend order and meaning to the data. Typologies, classificatory schemes, and taxonomies can also help problem-solvers categorize phenomena by highlighting their similarities and differences, and surveys can be used to determine attitudes, values, and beliefs among colleagues, research groups, managers, and the general population with regard to administrative procedures, requirements, performance, and the like.

All of these techniques, however, have many of their own special data, expertise, time, and support requirements which must be seriously considered before a descriptive analysis is undertaken.

For example, since statistical profiling techniques require large amounts of empirical or subjective quantitative data, problem-solvers should be aware of the time, money, and other costs connected with data collection and use. However, since all of the descriptive statistical techniques are accessible via simple-to-use computer programs, there is little processing and calculation support necessary. Similarly, all survey-based problem-solving is time- and labor-intensive. Typologies, taxonomies, and classificatory schemes can, however, be constructed *relatively* easily.

BIBLIOGRAPHIC ESSAY

Sources regarding the use of descriptive statistics include Hubert M. Blalock's *Social Statistics* (New York: McGraw-Hill, 1960), Henry F. DeFrancesco's *Quantitative Analysis Methods for Substantive Analysts* (Los Angeles: Melville, 1975), and D.J. Champion's *Basic Statistics for Social Research* (Scranton, PA: Chandler Publishing, 1970). Similarly, P. Games and G. Klare's *Elementary Statistics* (New York: McGraw-Hill, 1967), and L.C. Freeman's *Elementary Applied Statistics* (New York: John Wiley, 1965) are excellent introductory texts. David K. Hildebrand, James D. Laing, and Howard Rosenthal's *Analysis of Ordinal Data* (Beverly Hills, CA: Sage Publications, 1977), H.T. Reynolds' *Analysis of Nominal Data* (Beverly Hills, CA: Sage Publications, 1977), and Frederick Hartwig and Brian E. Dearing's *Explanatory Data Analysis* (Beverly Hills, CA: Sage Publications, 1979) represent three relatively short but very useful monographs on the many nuances of applied statistical analysis.

Survey research texts are also numerous and generally quite useful. For example, Earl R. Babbie's *The Practice of Social Research* (Belmont, CA: Wadsworth, 1975) and Charles H. Backstrom and Gerald D. Hursh's *Survey Research* (Evanston, Ill: Northwestern University Press, 1963) represent two highly readable applied sources, as do Leslie Kish's *Survey Sampling* (New York: John Wiley, 1965) and Robert L. Kahn and Charles F. Connell's *The Dynamics of Interviewing* (New York: John Wiley, 1965).

Finally, Babbie's *Practice of Social Research* and E. Tiryokian's "Typologies" (*International Encyclopedia of the Social Sciences*, 15, 1968, pp. 177–86) present two brief but informative looks at the application of classification techniques.

5

Explanation

WHEN A problem-solver is asked, or needs, to explain why and how phenomena occur the way they do, he or she will probably sit back and ponder the problem in some more or less causal or deterministic ways. After several hours (or days, weeks, or even months) of thought, discussion, and reading, an answer may emerge. When and if it does it will very often be narrative in form and unsystematic in content. Too frequently, the answer may become the basis for a change in policy or the creation of sets of brand new policies.

Regardless of how an explanatory problem is approached methodologically, it should always be structured via some form of modeling and, ideally, hypothesis formation, since relationships among variables or factors are generally the objects of analysis.

Usually, when such problem-structuring is properly constructed, more systematic methods will emerge as necessary alternatives to the intuitive-narrative one described above. The first of these methods is correlation.

CORRELATION

As discussed in chapter 4, two interval variables can be measured against one another in order to determine how positively or negatively they interrelate. Some variations of these interrelationships can be displayed in scatter plots, or scatter diagrams, as suggested in figures 5.1, 5.2, 5.3, and 5.4. The scatter plot in Figure 5.1 suggests a very stong positive correlation between two hypothetical variables: as the value of X increases so does the value of Y. Figure 5.2 suggests a near zero correlation between the variables, and Figure 5.3 presents a perfectly uncorrelated pair of variables. Figure 5.4 suggests a negative correlation where the value of Y decreases as the value of X increases.

The degree of association between the variables can be measured by the product moment correlation coefficient, almost always symbolized by the symbol r. Looking again at Figure 5.1, r measures the extent one can describe a bivariate relationship by a straight line. Given that r varies from +1.0 to -1.0, Figure 5.1 approximates r = +1.0, while Figure 5.4 approximates $r = -1.0$. It is extremely important to remem-

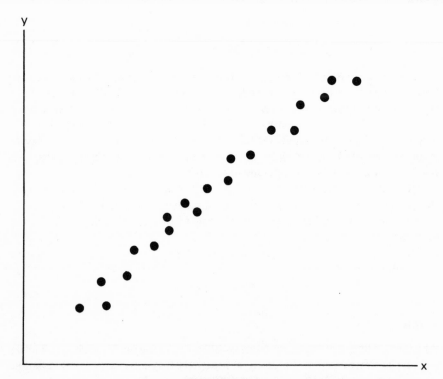

FIGURE 5.1
STRONG POSITIVE CORRELATION

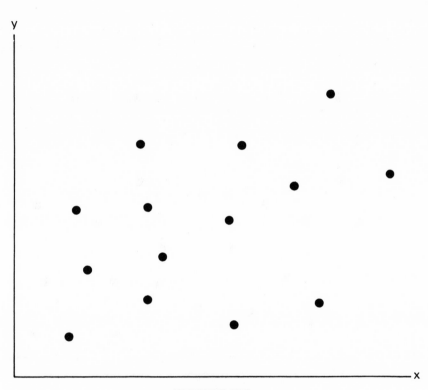

FIGURE 5.2
NEAR-ZERO CORRELATION

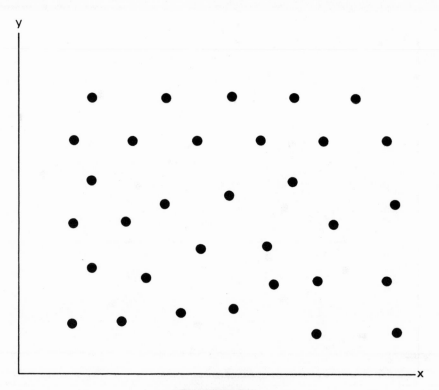

FIGURE 5.3
ZERO CORRELATION

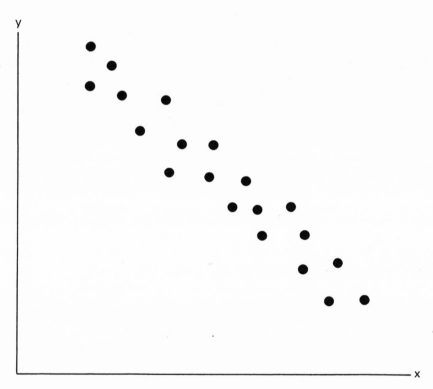

FIGURE 5.4
STRONG NEGATIVE CORRELATION

ber that the product moment correlation coefficient does not suggest causality. More-over, one must remember that an r of $-.75$ represents a stronger correlation than an r of $+.70$, since the $+$ or $-$ before a coefficient only refers to the direction of the re-lationship, not its degree. Accordingly, an r of $+1.0$ is as "strong" as an r of -1.0, though each says something very different about the direction of the relationship. Finally, r values cannot be interchanged or multiplied in order to derive additional or comparative r values: an r of $+.80$ does not equal two r values of $+.40$ or four of $+.20$.

In order to compare coefficients, one must compute what is known as a coeffi-cient of determination (r^2), which measures the amount of variance necessary in one variable to account for a change in the other. For example, an r value of $+.70$, while very positive, yields a coefficient of determination of only $.49$ $(+.70^2)$. In this ex-ample, then, one could have claimed to have "explained" less than half of the vari-ance between the two variables! Table 5.1 runs through an entire example of corre-lation between the variables salesperson age and sales using the standard equation for the calculation of the correlation coefficient.

Correlation can be used to "solve" a variety of analytical problems. It can be used to examine hypotheses about the interrelationships of variables. It can be used as a very preliminary step in the search for causes; and it can be used to test for third-variable impact, as suggested in Figure 5.5, which presents some "spurious" relation-ships. For example, while the number of fire engines might correlate very positively with the amount of fire damage, it is the size of the fire which actually explains both the number of fire engines and amount of damage. Consequently, one must be extremely careful when correlating variables to look for the impact of a third variable, which, when removed, may erase the relationship between the two initial variables.

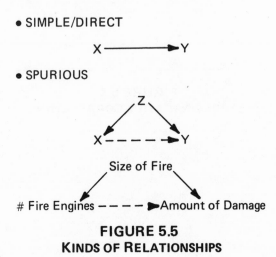

• SIMPLE/DIRECT

X   Y

• SPURIOUS

Z

X − − − − → Y

Size of Fire

Fire Engines − − − − ► Amount of Damage

FIGURE 5.5
KINDS OF RELATIONSHIPS

TABLE 5.1
SALESPERSON AGE/SALES CORRELATION COEFFICIENT

Age(x)	Sales(y)	x^2	y^2	xy
60	190	3600	36100	11400
58	192	3364	36864	11136
56	190	3136	36100	10640
54	170	2916	28900	9180
52	160	2704	25600	8320
50	160	2500	25600	8000
44	140	1936	19600	6160
40	100	1600	10000	4000
38	92	1444	8464	3496
34	69	1156	4761	2346
32	62	1024	3844	1984
30	46	900	2116	1380
29	40	841	1600	1160
24	29	576	841	696
21	10	441	100	210
$\Sigma x = 622$	$\Sigma y = 1650$	$\Sigma x^2 =$	$\Sigma y^2 =$	$\Sigma(xy) =$
$\bar{x} = 41.4$	$\bar{y} = 110$	28138	240490	80108

Correlation Coefficient $(r) =$

$$\frac{\Sigma xy - n(\bar{x}\bar{y})}{\sqrt{[\Sigma x^2 - n(\bar{x})^2]\ [\Sigma y^2 - n(\bar{y})^2]}} =$$

$$\frac{80108 - 15(41.4 \times 110)}{\sqrt{[28138 - 15(41.4)^2]\ [240490 - 15(110)^2]}} = .99$$

As with all of the statistical techniques discussed in chapter 4, correlation coefficients, and coefficients of determination, as well as many other measures of correlation not discussed here (such as biserial correlation, phi and tetrachoric coefficients, and correlation ratios), are all quite easily calculated via many easy-to-use computer programs available on a time-shared or dedicated basis (see chapter 11). Yet while the mechanics of calculation may be within easy reach, the necessary talent to implement the techniques properly may not. Similarly, data collection and formatting support requirements are also usually high when correlation analyses are conducted.

REGRESSION

Bivariate linear regression is a statistical technique for measuring the relationship between two variables presumed to be related in a way which yields measurable changes in one variable as a function of another. Thus, instead of using a scatter plot to determine a correlation between two variables, one can more precisely determine the form of a bivariate relationship by developing a straight line through a scatter plot. An example of such a linear relationship appears in Figure 5.6. Note that changes in the independent variable, X, result in predictable changes in the dependent variable, Y. In the example, which illustrates the application of the linear equation $Y = aX$, two lines have been drawn which represent the linear relationships of two variables given differing $a$lpha parameters.

Linear regression rests upon the positing and discovery of such linear relationships. Unlike correlation, which gives a measure of how positively or negatively two variables co-vary, regression permits one to predict Y from what is known about X *and* measure the difference between the actual and posited straight line (linear) relationship.

Regression analyses can be used to explain and predict salaries (Y) according to changes in employee age (X) based on prior experience, to explain and predict the occurrence of coups (Y) according to civil outbursts (X), and to explain and predict the sales (Y) of employees based upon their ages (X).

The formula for computing a regression coefficient is presented in an example in Table 5.2. In the example, the relationship between sales and age is once again examined, but note how the regression equation can tell what the effect of each increase in X (age) will be upon Y (sales). Correlation analysis was only able to tell how strongly and in what direction the two variables co-varied.

Regression can be used to explain and predict (see chapter 6) all kinds of events and conditions when—and only when—adequate quantitative data, talent, and computer support are all available. It is a powerful tool that has been computerized over and over again, but most notably in the computerized statistical package for the social sciences, SPSS (see chapter 11).

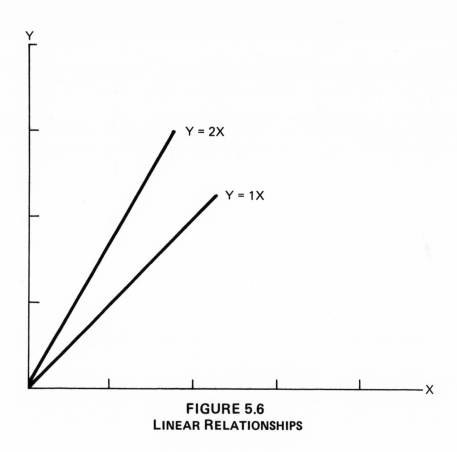

FIGURE 5.6
LINEAR RELATIONSHIPS

TABLE 5.2
SALESPERSON AGE/SALES REGRESSION COMPUTATION

Age (x)	Sales (y)	x^2	y^2	xy
49	16	2401	256	784
46	19	2116	361	874
60	19	3600	361	1140
36	11	1296	121	396
38	12	1444	144	456
56	13	3136	169	728
29	7	841	49	203
24	8	576	64	192
39	10	1521	100	390
58	17	3364	289	986
$\Sigma x = 435$	$\Sigma y = 132$	$\Sigma x =$	$\Sigma y =$	$\Sigma(xy) =$
$\bar{x} = 43.5$	$\bar{y} = 132$	20295	1914	6149

$$Y = a + bX \quad \longrightarrow \quad b = \frac{Exy - N\bar{x}\bar{y}}{\Sigma x^2 - [(\Sigma x)^2 / N]}$$

$$b = \frac{6149 - 10(43.5 \times 13.2)}{20295 - (435)^2 / 10} = .30^*$$

Every unit increase in X (age) will result in a .30 increase in Y (sales)

* In order to compute the regression line, a, the Y intercepts must be determined

MULTIPLE CORRELATION AND REGRESSION

Up to this point in this chapter and in chapter 4, we have concentrated upon the description and explanation of changes in one or two variables. It is of course possible to discover, describe, explain, and predict the relationships among many variables. For example, while age may correlate very positively with sales success, it may well be that sales region and time on the job also correlate highly with sales success. A multiple correlation or regression analysis would be able to tell how strongly each variable correlated with sales success and, in the case of a regression analysis, enable one to predict how changes in any of the independent variables (age, region, and experience) will impact upon the dependent variable (sales success).

In multiple regression, the basic formula remains the same as for bivariate regression, but additional independent variables are added to account for what is expected to be a "shared" effect upon the dependent variable:

$$Y = a + b_1 X_1 + b_2 X_2 + \ldots b_n X_n$$

But beware of multiple regression equations with more than five independent variables, because the variables themselves may be highly interrelated and therefore unable to yield an explicit impact upon the dependent variable. Since the regression process subtracts from the dependent variable the correlations among the independent variables, highly interrelated independent variables will not correlate as strongly with the dependent variable as unrelated ones.

Multiple correlation and regression can be used to describe, explain, and predict the precise interrelationships among variables when such variables are intuitively expected to correlate; but the techniques can also be used to discover relationships which may not be immediately obvious. Multiple correlation and regression can thus be used to discover, verify, *and* measure relationships.

CAUSAL MODELING

Figure 5.7 suggests three kinds of relationships. We have already discussed bivariate and multivariate relationships but have only done so in the simplest terms. Sometimes, however, events and conditions are not so easily modeled, and complex models must be developed.

Formal causal models are those which map complex relationships among individual or groups of variables in ways which explicitly recognize causal paths among the variables. Figure 5.8 presents a causal model of voting behavior. Note how the variables of party identification, issue positions, and candidate evaluation all interact to impact upon the vote itself, or the dependent variable in the model (also known as an "arrow diagram").

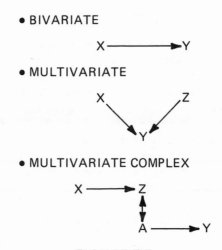

FIGURE 5.7
SIMPLE AND COMPLEX RELATIONSHIPS

Causal models are appropriately developed when a relatively large set of independent variables can be expected to have a traceable yet indirect impact upon a dependent variable. Statistical techniques, like path analysis, can calculate this impact and verify the assumptions in the causal model.

It is important to remember, however, that "causal" models attempt to capture relationships that may or may not be causal. Conceptually, because so many variables can be included in a causal model, there is a tendency to regard the model as comprehensive and therefore completely explanatory. In reality, all models are to some extent incomplete; causal models are thus "causal" only to the extent that they capture reality. The real basis of a causal model lies in its ability to visually (and then statistically) measure any number of direct and indirect relationship patterns and to what extent these patterns impact upon one (or more) dependent variable(s). At the same time, the development and use of causal models of all kinds is an extremely complicated and time-consuming undertaking. Even with computer support, causal models are seldom easy to use because an enormous amount of information about the problem must be known in order to properly construct them, and then, once constructed, an equally large amount of statistical expertise must be available in order to understand how to interpret the analytical results. Finally, there are really relatively few *applied* occasions when the development and use of causal models is absolutely necessary, and on those occasions when causal models might be profitably used, it should be determined if the marginal utility of using such a complicated procedure is justified given the requirements of the explanatory or predictive problem at hand. Often it will be discovered that the use of causal models cannot be justified on a cost-effectiveness basis.

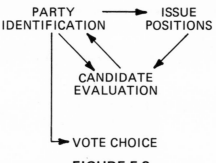

FIGURE 5.8
VOTING BEHAVIOR CAUSAL MODEL

STATISTICAL SIGNIFICANCE

Whenever complicated statistical concepts are implemented in an effort to describe, explain, or predict how two or more variables are likely to interact, efforts must be made to determine how significant statistically the results are, that is, how likely they were to occur by chance. The more significant the results the less likely they occurred by chance. While significance tests can be easily conducted via the same computer programs which facilitate rapid univariate, bivariate, and multivariate analyses, it is important to report tests results whenever statistical analyses are conducted and integrated into larger problem-solving processes. Not infrequently very strong—but statistically insignificant—results are generated by eager analysts who must suffer through the agony of either discarding the analyses or reporting analyses which must be very carefully—if at all—used.

SUMMARY

Correlation and regression are powerful and complicated explanatory techniques. They are not to be used by novices or under conditions where suport, time, and talent are in short supply.

They are also techniques which may or may not be appropriate to explanatory problems. Problem-solvers must assess all of the problem-solving conditions before undertaking their use.

Obviously data and computer support are necessary prerequisites to the successful use of correlation and regression. Without them, they will be of little problem-solving use. At the same time, since correlation and regression techniques have been computerized successfully in so many hardware/software configurations, they are now more accessible than they ever have been. Moreover, some of the better computer programs will provide on-line tutorials to prospective users.

Correlation and regression can be used to examine the relationship between two or more variables. But avoid analyses of more than five independent variables because usually they will be interrelated to an extent that will otherwise mask their measurable impact upon the dependent variable. Causal models can help organize variables to minimize such problems, but are extremely difficult to use productively. Finally, whenever complicated statistical routines are used to solve descriptive or explanatory problems, statistical significance tests must be conducted. Other statistical issues must also be addressed when quantitative data is collected and statistically manipulated.

BIBLIOGRAPHIC ESSAY

It is very difficult to suggest sources for correlation and regression because success with a particular source depends upon one's existing level of statistical knowledge. It must be understood that if one's level of statistical knowledge is quite low, then a good deal of time may have to be invested in order to grasp and apply the statistical concepts.

It is also extremely helpful to seek in-depth instruction in the correlation and regression areas. This, however, may or may not involve formal classes; sometimes just listening and observing others can be very instructive.

Finally, SPSS and other interactive (and batch) computer programs can ease many of the burdens connected with learning about and applying statistical techniques.

With the above in mind, Earl R. Babbie's *The Practice of Social Research* (Belmont, CA: Wadsworth, 1975) is again excellent, as are H.M. Blalock, Jr.'s edited *Causal Models in the Social Sciences* (Chicago: Aldine-Atherton, 1971) and his *Social Statistics* (New York: McGraw-Hill, 1960); Robert Brown's *Explanation in Social Science* (Chicago: Aldine-Atherton, 1963); M. Ezekiel and Karl Fox's *Methods of Correlation and Regression Analysis* (New York: John Wiley & Sons, 1959); and D.R. Heise's *Causal Analysis* (New York: John Wiley, 1975).

Two very good introductory texts include Michael S. Lewis-Beck's *Applied Regression: An Introduction* (Beverly Hills, CA: Sage Publications, 1980), and Allen L. Edwards' *An Introduction to Linear Regression and Correlation* (San Francisco: W.H. Freeman, 1976).

Herbert F. Spirer's *Business Statistics: A Problem-Solving Approach* (Homewood, Ill: Irwin, 1975), and Morris Hamburg's *Statistical Analysis for Decision Making* (New York: Harcourt, Brace and World, 1970) both discuss correlation and regression in specific problem-solving contexts.

Finally, many of the sources listed in chapter 4's Bibliographic Essay are again relevant here. Chapter 11's Bibliographic Essay lists some of the computer programs available for the conduct of correlation and regression analyses.

6

Prediction
and Forecasting

A GREAT many of the problems which face analysts, decision-makers, and managers are to some extent connected with the prediction and fore-casting of future events and conditions. Often such forecasts are required of and unto themselves; but more frequently forecasts are necessary in order to inform some other analytical function.

It would be a terrible understatement to suggest that the forecasting literature is voluminous. Literally thousands of articles, books, and monographs abound within academic, corporate, and countless governmental libraries. Nearly all of this litera-ture is concerned with the presentation and explanation of specific methods and less with how and when to apply such methods.

In order to engage in forecasting, however, one must first appreciate some of the components of the forecasting process itself. These include an understanding of the goals of forecasting, the objects of forecasting, as well as of course the methods of forecasting.

GOALS

It is essential that problem-solvers understand that forecasts and predictions may be distinguished according to their ranges. Specifically, there are short-range forecasts, medium-range forecasts, long-range forecasts, and even retrospective forecasts. Un-fortunately, there is no common definition about what constitutes a short- versus long-range forecast. To some, a short-range forecast extends out sixty days or less. Others regard one year as a short-range forecast. In the business community, for ex-ample, a long-range forecast is generally one which extends no farther than three years in time. But in the government, especially in the strategic defense area, a long-range forecast may extend well beyond twenty years into the future. It is important, then, that a specific definition be agreed upon during the organization and problem-identification phases of the problem-solving process.

In addition to forecasting ranges, problem-solvers should also distinguish between positive and negative forecasting goals. Positive and negative forecasts are concerned with what will and with what will not happen, respectively. Finally, problem-solvers should distinguish between objective and normative forecasts. Objective forecasts present what will be, while normative ones suggest what ought to be.

Most problems require forecasts that are objective, positive, and short-range in nature. When information is sparse, or talent unavailable, negative and retrospective forecasting may be used to enhance more positive future-oriented ones. Normative forecasting is more frequently the preoccupation of planners.

OBJECTS

Problem-solvers should also distinguish among possible forecasting objects. For example, event forecasting is by definition and nature more specific and precise than the forecasting of conditions. It is also important to distinguish between events and conditions which occur within or outside of the particular environments which are the objects of forecasting.

An understanding of the goals and objects of forecasting generally will inform and accelerate the particular requirements analysis process which should be conducted before the selection and implementation of a forecasting method. In fact, forecasting goal and object categories can be used to elicit requirements from problem-generators and solution-consumers. For example, goals could be used to define precisely the required forecasting range, while explicit attention to forecasting objects can direct the subsequent analysis toward defined events and conditions.

METHODS

Probably the most important forecasting task is the selection of the most appropriate method (or methods). Broadly, there are two primary forecasting methods: subjective and objective.

Subjective forecasting methods, by and large, are those which rely principally upon data or information generated by individual experts in the form of structured or unstructured opinions and/or judgments. Sometimes, subjective methods are referred to as "consensus methods" because they frequently rely upon the consensus judgments of the experts who generate a forecast. J. Scott Armstrong, a noted forecasting methodologist, refers to subjectively generated forecasts as implicit, informal, clinical, experience-based, intuitive, "guestimates," or gut feelings.

Armstrong goes on to assert that objective methods are those that use well-specified processes to analyze data. Ideally, in Armstrong's and many other methodologists' views, such processes have been specified so well that other problem-solvers can replicate them and obtain the same forecasts. Objective methods have also been called explicit, statistical, or "formal."

Interestingly, most forecasts are generated via subjective methodology and management research seems to indicate that the more important the forecast the greater is the likelihood that subjective methodology will be used.

Frequently methodologists attempt to argue that subjective methods never involve causal assertions about the phenomena to be forecast. This is simply not true. Highly structured subjective forecasting methods might very well require the use of a causal model or framework.

The only real distinction between the general methodologies lies with how the (subjective and/or objective) forecasting data is elicited. Subjective forecasting methods generally look to the "wisdom" or judgment of experts, while more objective ones generally rely upon forecasts generated via statistical routines of one kind or another. Again, however, this is not to say that subjective data and subjective forecasting is in no way scientific or statistical; rather, it is to argue that subjective methods generate forecasts essentially from the minds of the experts, while objective ones rely upon statistical manipulations of the data which is generally generated by observing empirical reality.

SUBJECTIVE METHODS

Those subjective forecasting methods which rely principally upon the *unstructured* wisdom or "expertise" of one or more experts are based upon an intuitive process which cannot be clearly described. However, while intuitive methods are not really methods at all, they can be effective, if not confusing and sometimes dangerous.

Delphi Methods

Other subjective methods are much more structured. Designed primarily to assist groups with the generation of forecasts, the *Delphi* method enables experts to exchange opinions about the likelihood of events and conditions. Specifically, the Delphi method can be implemented by mail or direct on-site anonymous questionnaires to recognized "experts." More than one "round" of judgments is always conducted and typically the experts are provided with the previous rounds' judgments as well as the rationale behind each judgment. For best results, the experts should not be assembled until the polling is completed. This will prevent the distortive influence of recognized and intimidating experts upon less notable experts and the Delphi process itself.

The Delphi method focuses forecasting opinions into an increasingly narrower range through the use of controlled feedback. The experts generally alter their prior responses somewhat when they read the responses of their colleagues. After enough rounds, the opinions usually converge into a single identifiable forecast.

A now famous Rand Corporation study, conducted by T.J. Gordon and Olaf Helmer and entitled *Report on a Long-Range Forecasting Study* (Santa Monica, CA: The Rand Corporation, P-2982, September 1964), will illustrate the Delphi process.

eighty-two "experts" participated in the study which sought to predict major possible scientific breakthroughs which might have occurred during the following 50 years, or during the period from 1964 to 2013. In the first round the participants listed the scientific breakthroughs judged to be possible and necessary within the 50-year time frame. Forty-nine items were listed, including reliable weather forecasts, molecular biology, and personality control drugs. In round two the same participants listed the probability of each of the 49 items occurring in the following time frames:

- ♦ 1964–65
- ♦ 1965–68
- ♦ 1968–72
- ♦ 1972–78
- ♦ 1978–86
- ♦ 1986–97
- ♦ 1997–2013
- ♦ Later than 2013
- ♦ Never

These probabilities were used to pinpoint the year the participants felt that the items had a 50% probability of occurring. For example, reliable weather forecasting was expected to occur by 1975 by 50% of the participants. In the third round the Delphi intermediary sent questionnaires to the participants requesting that those who did not agree with the general (50/50) consensus state why. Rationale requests were also made regarding the items on which there was little or no consensus. This round resulted in a narrowing of the estimates. The last round narrowed the time estimates even further. In fact, after the fourth round a consensus existed for 31 of the 49 items.

When time is short, a "mini-Delphi" can be conducted by performing some front-end work. According to procedures outlined by Mitchell, et. al in their *Handbook of Forecasting Techniques* (Menlo Park, CA: Stanford Research Institute, December 1975), before assembling the experts, decide upon the forecasting objects and goals. For example, if you need to predict the technologies most likely to affect the computer industry over the next 10 years, list the possible set before selecting the experts. Then prepare an index card for each of the technologies on which you should include a definition of each technology. Each expert should then randomly receive a numbered set of cards which he or she should then arrange according to their likely impact upon the computer industry. It is also a good idea to ask the experts to provide a rationale for their rankings. Next have the experts weight the technologies by assigning a percentage to each one according to how likely it is—in relation to the technology ranked above it—to positively affect the computer industry. According to this procedure, then, the most important technology would receive a score of 100%. The importance of the second most important technology would then be judged relative to the first and so on down the line. When all of the experts have ranked and weighted the technologies, the cards are collected and the information is aggregated.

Table 6.1 suggests how the experts' judgments can be converted into points. The total for each set of cards should be 1000. The first round of the mini-Delphi is thus completed when all of the points from all of the experts are totalled and a composite technology ranking is generated.

The experts are then given the results of the first round, and, after a face-to-face discussion of the results, the experts are asked to rethink their first-round judgments. The second-round judgments are then calculated. The results of this round should yield a "consensus"; if not, then another round may be necessary.

The Delphi and mini-Delphi forecasting techniques enjoy frequent use in government and industry. The Delphi technique is, however, somewhat difficult to implement. First, it is time-consuming and logistically complicated. Questionnaires must be designed, reproduced, and mailed out or personally distributed. Frequently, the

TABLE 6.1
MINI-DELPHI CALCULATIONS

"Expert" Judgments		Calculations	
Technology Rankings	% Weights	Weight Scale	Number of Points
1	100%	100%	319
2	90% ×	90%	288
3	70% ×	63%	201
4	60% ×	42%	134
5	30% ×	18%	58
		313%	1000

100% × 100%
90% × 100%
70% × 90% $\frac{1000}{313} = 3.19$
60% × 70%
30% × 60%

3.19 × 100%
3.19 × 90%
3.19 × 63%
3.19 × 42%
3.19 × 18%

participants do not return the questionnaires on time. Questionnaires also sometimes come back filled out improperly or incompletely. Considerable support is also necessary to analyze and compute the responses. Obviously, the mini-Delphi technique is easier to implement, but, because of its non-anonymonic nature, is not as precise as the formal Delphi method.

More general strengths and weaknesses include Delphi applicability to forecasting problems which are "fuzzy," that is, which defy precise definition. Delphi can also be used productively when it is not possible or economically feasible to bring all of the experts together for face-to-face discussions or mini-Delphis. Also, while sometimes cumbersome, Delphis are relatively inexpensive and versatile.

The general problems include finding enough appropriate experts, developing a sophisticated questionnaire, and reifying the results of the questionnaire. In short, it is a good idea to regard Delphi forecasts not as precise statements about the likelihood of specific events or conditions, but as subjective approximations of the future.

In summary, Delphi methods are implemented via procedures which require:

- ◆ The use of Experts
- ◆ Multiple Rounds of Inquiry
- ◆ Feedback

Formal Delphi Techniques require anonymity among geographically distributed participants; mini-Delphi exercises can be conducted with experts who interact face to face. While both procedures require reporting anonymity, the face-to-face mini-Delphi exercise is more affected by the personalities of the experts because of the face-to-face discussions which follow each round.

Bayesian Methods

Still another subjective forecasting methodology relies upon the use of *Bayes' theorem of conditional probabilities.* The three variations of Bayesian forecasting discussed below include simple Bayesian updating, probability diagramming, and hierarchial inference structuring. At the core of all three variations is the use of Bayes' theorem for revising a probability in the light of new information.

From a practical perspective, and by way of illustrating how a forecasting problem can be "solved" via the use of Bayes' theorem, consider that when an individual approaches a forecasting problem he or she generally has some opinion about the likelihood of the future event(s) or condition(s) in question. This "prior opinion" is then revised as new information is gathered or received to produce a "new" opinion. For example, if one were expected to forecast the price of OPEC crude in six months, one would, based upon the information at hand, forecast a particular price per barrel. Ideally, one would assign a "confidence," or probability, to the forecast. As new information was received, the forecast would rise or fall depending upon how the forecaster integrated the new information into his or her mental model of OPEC crude oil pricing.

While this unstructured process is sometimes effective, it is not as systematic as is could be. Bayes' theorem of conditional probabilities can breathe rigor into the process by specifying how prior opinion can be revised in the light of new information:

$$\frac{P(H_1/D_1)}{P(H_2/D_1)} = \frac{P(D_1/H_1)}{P(D_1/H_2)} \cdot \frac{P(H_1)}{P(H_2)}$$

where

H	=	hypotheses or explanations of information
D	=	data or information
$P(D_1/H_1)$	=	the probability that a piece of data or information, D_1, would be observed assuming that hypothesis one, H_1, is true
$P(H_1/D_1)$	=	the probability that hypothesis one, H_1, is true assuming that a piece of information, D_1, has been observed
$P(H_1)$	=	the forecaster's initial or prior opinion that hypothesis one, H_1, is true, i.e., before D_1 is considered
$\dfrac{P(D_1/H_1)}{\overline{P(D_1/H_1)}}$	=	the likelihood ratio, i.e., the forecaster's relative judgment regarding the likelihood that a piece of data or information would be observed given that the first hypothesis, H_1, is true over the second hypothesis, H_2
$\dfrac{P(H_1)}{P(H_2)}$	=	the prior odds that H_1 is true over H_2, i.e., the odds before a piece of data or information is considered

In application, the forecaster first estimates the prior odds which might be set equally (1:1) if great uncertainty about the hypotheses exists. The forecaster then considers the first piece of new information and estimates the first likelihood ratio. When the prior odds are multiplied by the likelihood ratio, revised or posterior odds are produced. These revised odds reflect the revised (probabilistic) opinion (about, for example, the probability of pricing) after new data has been considered. As more information is received and/or generated, the steps are repeated to produce successive revised odds.

Returning to the OPEC pricing problem, imagine a forecaster responsible for determining whether or not the price of a barrel of OPEC crude oil will rise above \$40 in six months. Three pieces of information now exist:

1. Uncharacteristically, the Saudi Arabians have made no announcements regarding their desire to hold crude oil prices down; in-

stead, they have announced a desire to modernize their nation and have made public their desire to invest billions in the modernization plan.

2. OPEC spokesmen announced that in recent years American currency has been devalued so dramatically that OPEC revenue has actually declined against 1977 calculations.

3. Western importing countries have abided by their agreement to hold oil import demands to 1978 levels; severe energy problems are beginning to diminish in the Western nations and alternative energy source development is proceeding on schedule; accordingly, the Western nations—primarily the United States—have concluded that future demand for OPEC crude oil can only be expected to diminish suggesting a budding energy independence.

Before the forecaster considers this information, he or she would estimate the prior odds against the two hypotheses:

H_1 – OPEC will keep prices below \$40 per barrel

H_2 – OPEC will raise the price of its crude oil above \$40 per barrel within six months.

The prior odds might be set at 1:1.5 by the forecaster who initially favors the second hypothesis. The first expression is thus:

$$\text{Prior Odds} = \frac{P(H_1)}{P(H_2)} = \frac{1}{1.5}$$

The first piece of information is then interpreted by the forecaster to suggest a price increase. More specifically, the forecaster determines that the likelihood of "observing" the absence of Saudi announcements regarding holding prices down and the announcement to embark upon an expensive modernization program is twice as likely if a price increase were imminent than if it were not. The posterior odds would thus be computed as follows:

$$\text{First Revised Odds} = \frac{P(D_1/H_1)}{P(D_1/H_2)} = \frac{1}{2} \cdot \frac{1}{1.5} = \frac{1}{3.0}$$

The odds favoring a price increase are now 3:1 based upon the consideration of one new piece of information.

The second piece of information is also determined to be diagnostic of a price increase, as estimated below:

$$\text{Second Revised Odds} = \frac{P(D_2/H_1)}{P(D_2/H_2)} = \frac{1}{10} \cdot \frac{1}{3} = \frac{1}{30}$$

At this point, then, the forecaster has determined that a price increase is 30 times more likely than not after having examined two pieces of information.

The third piece of information is interpreted as favoring stable prices:

$$\text{Third Revised Odds} = \frac{P(D_3/H_1)}{P(D_3/H_2)} = \frac{5}{1} \cdot \frac{1}{30} = \frac{1}{6}$$

After observing three pieces of information, the forecaster concludes that a price increase is six times as likely as <$40 per barrel pricing, i.e., the probability of an increase is 0.834, and 0.166 of a <$40 per barrel price.

Obviously, the above example is unrealistically simple. Yet, it does illustrate how the formal mathematical structure of Bayes' theorem can be used as a probabilistic forecasting tool. Normally, more than two hypotheses are scrutinized and several hundred pieces of information are considered. (A forecaster would also want to integrate reliability assessments of observed information into the information processing.)

Some of the advantages associated with the use of this fundamental Bayesian forecasting technique include, first, the efficient extraction of diagnostic certainty from generated or available information. If each piece of information is interpreted diagnostically, then—theoretically at least—less information will be required to generate a forecast and, relatedly, forecasts can be generated more rapidly. In addition, while it was not immediately evident above, the use of Bayes' theorem enables forecasts to be generated by individuals and by groups of forecasters. Since the theorem is disconnected from the assessments made by the forecaster(s), it proposes one solution to the problem of human information overload. If a single individual—or even several individuals—cannot cognitively process all of the incoming information pertinent to the forecasting problem, the Bayesian methodology readily permits the addition of as many forecasters as are needed to solve the problem.

A more detailed example presents some of the advantages via a "log odds" chart to display revised probabilities in a convenient, easily assimilated manner. When both sides of the Bayesian equation are converted to logarithms, the log of the posterior odds equals the log of the prior odds and the log of the likelihood ratio. In logarithmic form, data, as represented by the log of the likelihood ratio, is unaffected by the prior odds. For example, if the log of the likelihood ratio is 0.5, and the prior log odds equal 0.0, then the posterior log odds will equal +0.5. On the log odds chart, the right vertical axis is scaled in log odds, the left vertical in probabilities, and the horizontal is scaled in time.

An example of log odds charting involves a retrospective analysis of the Soviet invasion of Czechoslovakia in 1968, which appears in Scott Barclay, et. al's *Handbook for Decision Analysis* (McLean, VA: Decisions and Design, Inc., September 1977). Two hypotheses were formulated relevant to the situation in Western Europe in 1968. The first hypothesis stated that within one year the Soviet Union will invade Czechoslovakia, while the second stated that within the same period of time the Soviet Union will not invade Czechoslovakia. Assume it is January, 1968 and that there is a body of information which exists in various forms that would enable a forecaster to arrive at some judgment regarding the likelihood of an invasion at that point in time. Such information might lead one to determine that there was one chance in 20 that the first hypothesis is true (or that there is a probability of 0.05 that H_1 is true and a probability of 0.95 that H_2 is true). The prior odds thus equal:

$$\text{Prior Odds} = \frac{P(H_1)}{P(H_2)} = \frac{1}{20}$$

As new information became available, it might have been assessed in the light of these prior odds. For example, consider the datum that might have been observed in February of 1968 regarding Brezhnev's visit to Czechoslovakia. Interpretations of that visit might have suggested that Brezhnev may have travelled to Czechoslovakia to exert pressure upon Dubcek. Such information could easily have been evaluated in the light of the two hypotheses. In this case, the forecaster would have to decide whether the visit had any bearing on the "truth" of H_1 and H_2. A forecaster might thus have assessed a probability of 0.80 that Brezhnev would visit Czechoslovakia if there were to be an invasion, and a probability of 0.50 that he would be there if there were to be no invasion. The likelihood ratio of the first datum is thus 0.80/0.50 = 1.6:1. The posterior probabilities would have been reflected by multiplying 1.6/1 (the likelihood ratio) by 1/20 (the prior odds), yielding posterior odds to 1:12.5. Next, consider four additional pieces of information relevant to the hypotheses, including: the visit of Marshall Ivan F. Yakubovsky of the Soviet Union, the commander of the Warsaw Pact military alliance in East Berlin, for talks with Walter Ulbricht, First Secretary of the Communist Party, on measures to reinforce the alliance's defense system (#2); the visit of Alexander Dubcek to Moscow for meetings with the Soviet government (#3); the announcement that the armed forces of the Warsaw Pact were to hold exercises on Czechoslovakian and Polish territory under the supervision of Marshall Ivan F. Yakubovsky (#4); and the announcement that Warsaw Pact maneuvers in Czechoslovakia would involve only selected command staffs of the various services (#5).

Interestingly enough, the next four pieces of data that might have been observed from June 30th to August 5th all included a decreasing amount of tension toward

Czechoslovakia. Such developments would have favored the first hypothesis, no invasion. For example, on June 30th the military staff exercises of Warsaw Pact forces which had created anxiety in Czechoslovakia ended (#6); on July 13th some of the Soviet troops still in Czechoslovakia two weeks after the end of the joint Warsaw Pact maneuvers started for home (#7); on July 30th, well-informed Czechoslovakian sources believed that the meeting between the leaders of Czechoslovakia and those of the Soviet Union had served to push the possibility of Soviet military intervention further into the background. Their belief was based on authoritative reports on new Soviet demands or threats (#8); and finally, the spector of "counterrevolution" in Czechoslovakia that evoked cries of outrage and alarm from the Soviet Union seemed in Moscow to have disappeared abruptly, and mass propaganda rallies throughout the country to stir up hostility against the Czechoslovakian liberation program ended by August 5th (#9).

The tenth, eleventh, twelfth, and thirteenth pieces of information reverse the downward trend and suggest that tension between the Soviets and the Czechs began to grow again after August 5th. The tenth piece of information, for example, revealed that the Soviet Communist Party warned its members against ideas about liberalization of the party along the line of the recent Czechoslovakian reforms. Number 11, received on August 16th, reported that the Soviet Union had resumed polemics against the Czechoslovakian press after a lapse of three weeks. Number 12 reported that the Soviet Communist Party expressed apprehension that the Czechoslovakian leadership appeared to be losing control in the country; Number 13, received on August 19th, reported that Czechoslovakian army divisions would exercise Wednesday and Thursday in Bohemia, with observers from other Warsaw Pact countries present.

Number 13 might have been the last piece of information considered. At that point, the likelihood ratio equalled 8.3/1. This raised the total posterior odds to 33:1, or to a probability of approximately 97 percent in favor of the first hypothesis. All of the information is presented in the figure on a log odds chart.

History, of course, informs us that the invasion occurred on August 20, 1968. The initial assessment of prior odds, which were 1:20 against the invasion, slowly increased until May 24th. At that time the odds were 3.9/1 in favor of H_1; after that time, four consecutive pieces of information suggested that the tension between the USSR and Czechoslovakia was easing; on August 5th, the likelihood of an invasion dropped to 1:6 (or only a 14 percent chance). On August 9th, however, just 11 days before an invasion, the Soviets resumed attacks against the Czechs. The attacks continued until the 19th when it was announced that exercises would be held in Czechoslovakia. At that time the total posterior odds rose to 33:1 (or a 97 percent probability of invasion). Figure 6.1 presents all of the assessments on a log odds chart.

Another way to deal with uncertainty is to develop a probability diagram, as shown in Figure 6.2. In the diagram, the forecaster is concerned with whether or not it will rain on the company picnic. Notice that the forecaster, an amateur weatherman, has decided that wind direction and barometric pressure will affect the likelihood of "rain" or "no rain."

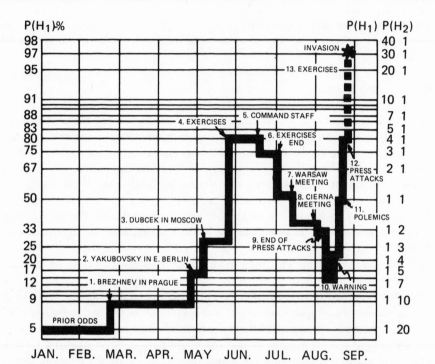

FIGURE 6.1
LOG ODDS CHARTING OF CZECHOSLOVAKIAN INVASION

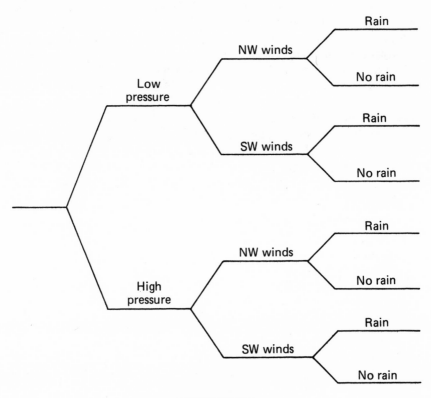

FIGURE 6.2
PROBABILITY DIAGRAM

In order to generate a useful forecast from a probability diagram, one must first be sure that all of the branches in the diagram are mutually exclusive, exhaustive, and sum to 1.0 or 100%. Figure 6.3 presents the forecaster's judgements across the probability diagram. In order to generate these probabilities the forecaster must assume that all of the antecedent events in the diagram have occurred. For example, the probability of rain (P_4) must be assessed assuming the occurrence of low barometric pressure and NW winds. The first probability (P_1) is an "unconditional" probability: it is dependent upon no other event or condition. But P_2, P_3, P_4, P_5, P_6, and P_7 are "conditional" probabilities, that is, dependent upon the occurrence of other events and conditions. The next step involves multiplying all of the probabilities along each path. In the example, the upper path probability is obtained by multiplying 0.80, 0.70, and 0.90 to produce a 0.504 (50.4%) path probability. It is important to understand, however, that all of the path probabilities represent the occurrence of all of the events along the paths, not any one or just the unconditional event. After the forecaster combines the event probabilities to generate the path probabilities, the individual (rain/no rain) probabilities must be added. In our example, the probability of rain equals (.504 + 0.168 + 0.048 + 0.024) 0.74 (74%), and the probability of no rain equals (0.056 + 0.072 + 0.032 + 0.096) 0.26 (26%).

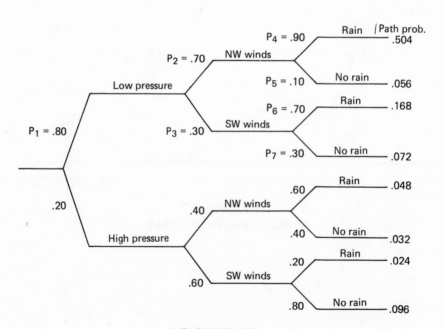

FIGURE 6.3
PROBABILITY DIAGRAM WITH FORECASTER'S JUDGEMENTS

Especially complicated forecasting problems which are either recurring or time-consuming require a methodology which is highly structured and highly diagnostic. The *hierarchical inference structuring technique* allows a forecaster to inferentially structure the relationships between predictor and target variables. The sequential nature of a hierarchical inference structure can be described schematically by a diagram called an inference tree. Figure 6.4 presents a generalized inference tree in which there are a number of (hierarchical) levels which rise to a set of hypotheses (H). These hypotheses sit at the top of the structure and are impacted by the activities (A), indicators (I), and data (D) which feed directly into them. The next level of the hierarchy is comprised of the indicators and data which impact upon the hypotheses through the second-level activities. As with the activities and data, each indicator and piece of data consists of a number of exhaustive, mutually exclusive states. The fourth and final level of the hierarchy is comprised of the data which impacts on the hypotheses via the indicators and activities on the third and second levels, respectively.

One of the best substantive examples, of how (and why) a hierarchical inference structure should be constructed may be found in Barclay, et. al *Handbook for Decision Analysis* (McLean, VA: Decisions and Designs, Inc., 1977). How does a forecaster determine if a country plans to develop a nuclear weapons production capability in five years? The first step is to generate the hypotheses which will sit at the top of the hierarchical structure;

H_1 – country A intends to develop a nuclear weapons production capability within five years

H_2 – country A does not intend to develop a nuclear weapons production capability within five years

The forecaster then lists the activities, indicators, and data which would support the hypotheses, and then organizes them into a hierarchical inference structure, as presented in Figure 6.5.

In order to make the structure "perform," the forecaster has to associate observable information probabilistically with the two hypotheses. These associations are conditional probabilities of the likelihood of observing data, indicators, and/or activities given the truth of the indicators, activities, and hypotheses, respectively.

Once the forecaster has completed the conditional probability assessment process for the entire hierarchical structure, he or she is in a position to construct what is known as a deductive hierarchical structure, as shown in Figure 6.6.

Now the problem must be "solved" from the bottom up, or inductively, as shown in Figure 6.7. The numbers in each box show the (relative) likelihood of

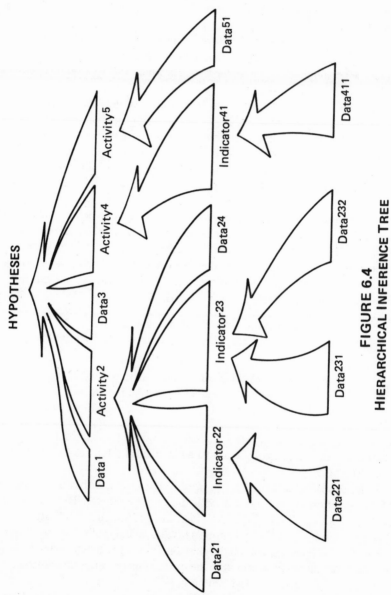

FIGURE 6.4
HIERARCHICAL INFERENCE TREE

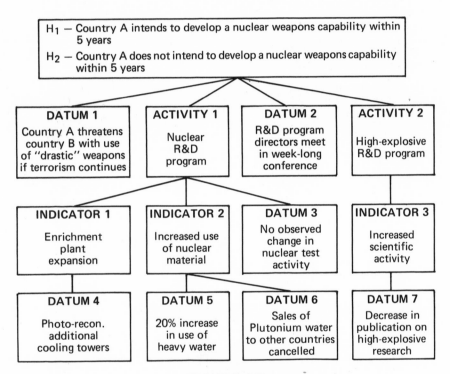

FIGURE 6.5
NUCLEAR WEAPONS PRODUCTION
HIERARCHICAL INFERENCE STRUCTURE

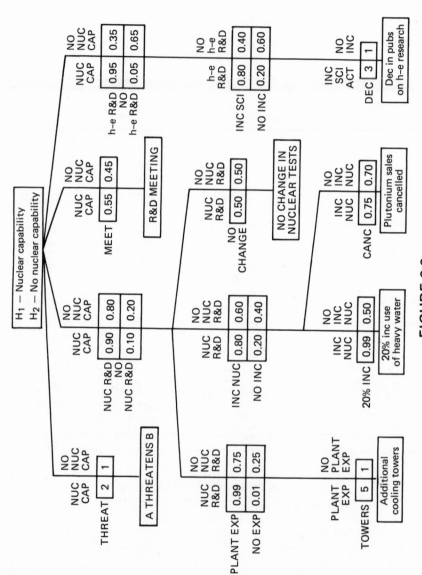

FIGURE 6.6

DEDUCTIVE HIERARCHICAL INFERENCE STRUCTURE

the data below that point in the structure, given the occurrence of the above level. The top of the inductive structure shows the final likelihood ratio, calculated as follows:

$$\frac{P(D/H_1)}{P(D/H_1)} = \frac{4.48}{1.45} = \frac{3.1}{1}$$

Given that prior odds were assessed as 1:1, posterior odds are calculated via the application of Bayes' theorem of conditional probabilities:

$$\frac{P(H_1/D)}{P(H_2/D)} = \frac{P(D/H_1)P(H_1)}{P(D/H_2)P(H_2)} = \frac{3.1}{1} \cdot \frac{1}{1} = \frac{3.1}{1}$$

After building and activating the deductive and inductive hierarchical structures, the forecaster concludes that there is a 76 percent probability that country A intends to develop a nuclear weapons production capability, a probability that would change as new information was brought to the problem.

As is obvious from the above example, the hierarchical inference structuring forecasting methodology is complicated and time consuming. While one need not worry about the problem of oversimplification with the adoption of the method, one must guard against building an unmanageable structure, one which is, in short, too big to use. Finally, given the resources necessary to apply the technique, the forecaster should also carefully select the forecasting problem to which to apply the method. Clearly, "one shot" or short-term forecasting problems are unsuited to hierarchical inference structuring. Conversely, problems which are recurring, long-term, and exceedingly complicated are probably best addressed by the hierarchical inference structuring technique.

One of the most useful aspects of the technique is that it structurally facilitates the focussing of different expert opinions at different parts of the structure. This aspect, in turn, facilitates group forecasting by exposing the many and varied components of the complicated forecasting problem.

In fact, all of the Bayesian, or probabilistic, forecasting methods facilitate the use of many different kinds of experts. Moreover, because the methods are subjective, they are explicit. However, as the above discussions suggest, the Bayesian methods can be tedious. Consequently, computer support is almost always necessary to implement them productively. The Bayesian methods are also time consuming and labor intensive (even with computer support.) Yet they remain popular, primarily because many managers and decision-makers still distrust heavily empirical analyses and because whatever the forecast it is traceable before, during, and after its issue.

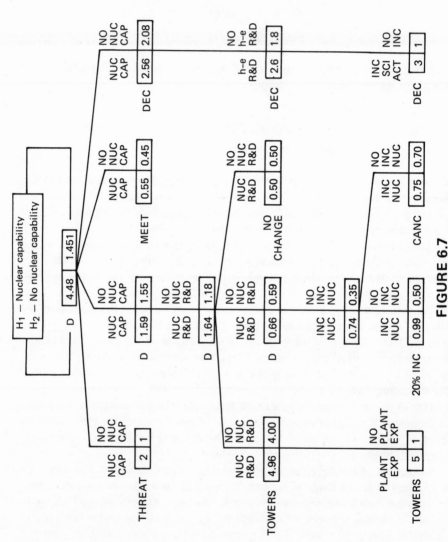

FIGURE 6.7

INDUCTIVE HIERARCHICAL INFERENCE STRUCTURE

In summary, there are at least three applied Bayesian methods which are all grounded in probability theory. They all also rely upon subjective or "expert" judgments and probability estimates, and herein lies their strength and weakness. The methods were also presented sequentially according to how difficult they are to use. Bayes' theorem of conditional probabilities is implemented rather easily, while hierarchical inference structuring is quite difficult to use. However, since all of the Bayesian methods have been computerized (see the Bibliographic Essay at the end of this chapter), they can all be implemented effectively given enough relative time, talent, and support. Again, the three Bayesian methods are:

♦ Bayes Theorem and Log/Odds Plotting

♦ Probability Diagramming

♦ Hierarchical Inference Structuring

Cross-Impact Methods

Another subjective forecasting method which relies upon the subjective estimates of experts is the cross-impact method. This method presumes that future events and conditions are interrelated. Most importantly, it attempts to determine probabilistically how a change in one event or condition will affect one or more other events or conditions.

In order to implement the cross-impact method one must take the following steps:

1. Assemble a group of knowledgeable experts with direct experience in the problem area under consideration.

2. Determine the forecasting goal.

3. List the events or conditions that might occur during the time period under consideration and which might exert an impact upon the forecasting object.

4. Estimate the probability of each event or condition occurring during the specified time period.

5. Construct a probability cross-impact matrix similar to the one presented in Figure 6.8.

6. Estimate the conditional or contingent probability for each paired set of events or conditions in the cross-impact matrix, as suggested in Figure 6.8.

7. Calculate (usually with computer support) the event or condition likelihoods given the initial event/condition and paired event/condition pair probabilities.

8. Evaluate results and then determine if additional estimates and calculations are necessary.

If This Event Occurs:	Initial Prob-ability	The Probability Of This Event Becomes:							
		1	2	3	4	5	6	7	8
Event 1		■							
Event 2			■						
Event 3				■					
Event 4					■				
Event 5						■			
Event 6							■		
Event 7								■	
Event 8									■

FIGURE 6.8
CROSS-IMPACT MATRIX

The main strength of the cross-impact is that it allows forecasters to estimate the likelihood of events or conditions based upon the likelihood of other events or conditions. Since it is also almost always computer-based, the cross-impact method can be implemented relatively easily. (However, in its manual form, the method is extremely difficult to implement effectively.) At the same time, like all of the forecasting methods discussed above, the cross-impact method is only as diagnostic as the estimates which fuel its implementation. Knowledgeable and responsible experts usually produce useful forecasts, but lazy ones will leave management very dissatisfied. Logistically, the cross-impact method—with computer support—can be implemented as easily as Delphi and Bayesian methods.

All of the subjective forecasting methods depend upon the quality of expert judgments and probability estimates which are converted methodologically into forecasts. Fortunately, they are all computer-based and fairly straightforward. In summary, the subjective forecasting methods presented above include the following:

- Delphi
- Bayesian

    Bayes Theorem and log/odds plotting
    Probability diagramming
    Hierarchical inference structuring

- Cross-Impact

OBJECTIVE METHODS

On the objective methodology side are extrapolative, inferential statistical, and econometric techniques.

Extrapolative Methods

Extrapolative methods generally fall into one of several categories. The first, and perhaps most widely used, form of extrapolation involves the conduct of persistence or consistent extrapolation. Persistence extrapolation assumes that any number of critical factors will persist over time and more or less contribute to a set of events or conditions which will occur sometime in the future. This kind of methodology is useful in predicting day-to-day developments, for it assumes these realities to be relatively unchanging.

Another type of extrapolation involves the extrapolative projection of trends. This method is used frequently for studies of technology, population, voting, and economic development. As a method, trend extrapolation is extremely easy to use, primarily because the assumptions underlying the methodology are easy to understand.

Yet another type of extrapolation is conducted by "acting out" the future in compressed time. Via computer or people simulations, this method can yield important insight into the future.

Still another form of extrapolative methodology involves the inventing of the future through the creation of complicated and uncomplicated scenarios. While these are popularly believed to be the product of intuitive or expert judgments, they can just as frequently be constructed through the use of empirical data.

Some of the specific tools surrounding extrapolative methodology include time series analysis, the calculation of moving averages, exponential smoothing, and pure trend projecting.

In moving average calculations, each point of a moving average of a time series is the arithmetic or weighted average of a number of consecutive points of the series where the number of data points is chosen so that the effects of seasonality or irregularity (or both) are eliminated. In order to successfully determine a moving average, a minimum of two years of prior data is usually necessary.

The exponential smoothing technique is similar to the moving average, except that more recent data points are given more weight. Descriptively, the new forecast is equal to the old one plus some proportion of the past forecasting error. Adaptive forecasting is somewhat the same except that seasonals are also computed. There are many variations of exponential smoothing; some are more versatile than others and some are computationally more complex. All require some computer time.

The Box-Jenkins technique is yet another kind of extrapolative forecasting methodology. In fact, exponential smoothing is a special case of the Box-Jenkins technique. The time series is fitted with an optimal mathematical model that assigns smaller errors to history than any other model. Many forecasters regard the Box-Jenkins technique as one of the most accurate statistical routines presently available; however, many others regard the technique as one of the most costly and time consuming.

The simple trend projective technique fits a trend line to a mathematical equation and then projects it into the future by means of the equation. There are several variations: the slope-characteristic, polynominal, and logarithmic methods.

All of the extrapolative techniques generally require a good deal of empirical data from which to extract the trends or projections necessary to produce a forecast. As a result, data and time costs may be considerable. Fortunately, a good many computer programs now exist which enable a forecaster to interactively conduct an extrapolative forecasting analysis of his or her choice easily, quickly, and efficiently.

Inferential Statistical Methods

In addition to methods based primarily upon extrapolative assumptions are those which are more causal in their orientation. These include the use of regression models, econometric models, input-output models, leading indicator approaches and methods, and life cycle analyses, among others.

As discussed in chapter 5, regression is a statistical technique for predicting one variable from knowledge of its association with other variables on the basis of past experience. A "dependent variable" is the event or condition the analyst or forecaster wishes to explain or predict. The "independent variable" is the one whose changes and fluctuations are used to explain or predict changes in the dependent variable.

Regression begins with correlation to determine the strength of association between two variables. It then describes the association by discovering which one or combination of variables correlates best with the dependent variable(s). This combination of variables reduces masses of data to equations that can be used to predict the dependent variable (see chapter 5).

Econometric Methods

An econometric model is a system of interdependent regression equations that describes a network of activity. The boundaries of the equations are usually estimated simultaneously. Unfortunately, econometric models are relatively expensive to develop.

An example of an econometric model of international conflict processes appears in Figure 6.9. Developed by Professor Nazli Choucri of the Massachusetts Institute of Technology ("Applications of Econometric Analysis to Forecasting in International Relations," *Peace Research Society International Papers*, 21, 1973, pp. 15-39), the model is very complex. Table 6.2 lists the model's equations.

As you can see, econometric forecasting is one of the most complex methods yet developed. Not only must several years of data be available to construct and exercise an econometric model, but one sophisticated with the development of simultaneous equations must also be available. It is not a quick and easy forecasting method to be implemented by the novice. Moreover, since the methodology itself is still under some development, significant questions can be raised regarding its overall utility.

As with the extrapolative techniques discussed above, these so-called causal techniques based largely upon the use of inferential statistics require large amounts of data and computer time. In addition, the statistical assumptions which underlie their use must be fully comprehended.

The many objective methods can be classified according to whether or not they fall into one of the following categories:

- ◆ Extrapolative Methods
- ◆ Inferential Statistical Methods
- ◆ Econometric Methods

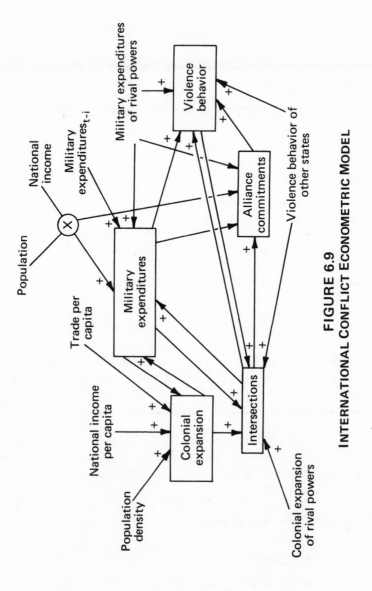

FIGURE 6.9
INTERNATIONAL CONFLICT ECONOMETRIC MODEL

TABLE 6.2
INTERNATIONAL CONFLICT ECONOMETRIC MODEL EQUATIONS

col-area	$= \alpha_1 + \beta_1$ h-pop/h-area $+ \beta_2$ nat-inc/h-pop $+ \beta_3$ trade/pop $+ \beta_4$ mil-exp $+ u_1$
intersections	$= \alpha_2 + \beta_5$ col-area $+ \beta_6$ mil-exp $+ \beta_7$ versus*non-allies' col-area $+ \beta_8$ viol-beh $+ \beta_9$ viol-others $+ u_2$
mil-exp	$= \alpha_3 + \beta_{10}$mil-exp$_{t-1}$ $+ \beta_{11}$ versus*non-allies' mil-exp $+ \beta_{12}$ intersections $+ \beta_{13}$ col-area $+ \beta_{14}$ h-pop*nat-inc $+ u_3$
alliances	$= \alpha_4 + \beta_{15}$ mil-exp $+ \beta_{16}$ intersections $+ \beta_{17}$ versus*non-allies' mil-exp $+ \beta_{18}$ h-pop*nat-inc $+ u_4$
viol-beh	$= \alpha_5 + \beta_{19}$ intersections $+ \beta_{20}$ mil-exp $+ \beta_{21}$ versus*non-allies' mil-exp $+ \beta_{22}$ alliances $+ \beta_{23}$ viol-others $+ u_5$
and	the co-terms for $\beta_4, \beta_5, \beta_6, \beta_8, \beta_{12}, \beta_{13}, \beta_{15}, \beta_{16}, \beta_{19}, \beta_{20}, \beta_{22}$, are endogenous variables, β_{10} is a lagged endogenous variable, and the co-terms for the other explanatory variables are exogenous,
col-area	= colonial area in thousand square miles
h-pop	= home population in thousand
h-area	= home area in thousand square miles
nat-inc	= national income in thousand U.S. dollars at standardized prices (1901–1910 = 100)
trade	= imports plus exports in thousand U.S. dollars at standardized prices (1901–1910 = 100)
mil-exp	= military expenditures (army and navy allocations) in thousand U.S. dollars at standardized prices (1901–1910 = 100)
versus*non-allies	= dummy variable representing dyadic relationship: 1 when two states are not allied formally, 0 if they are
intersections	= scaled variable (from 1 to 30) denoting intensity of intersections among spheres of influence
alliances	= number of alliance commitments
viol-beh	= scaled variable (from 1 to 30) denoting the highest peak on the scale recorded for each year, and representing the behavior of the actor *toward* other states
viol-others	= scaled variable (from 1 to 30) denoting the highest peak on the scale recorded for each year and representing the behavior of other states *toward* the actor state
h-pop*nat-inc	= multiplicative variable representing interactive effect of population (in thousands) and national income (in thousand U.S. dollars standardized to U.S. dollars, 1901–1910 = 100)
$\alpha_1 \ldots \alpha_5$	= constant or intercept term
$u_1 \ldots u_5$	= error or disturbance term

instrumental variable list: volume of iron and steel production, volume of pig iron, government expenditures, merchant marine tonnage, military expenditures of non-allies, colonial area of non-allies, population density, population times national income, national income per capita, trade per capita, intersections$_{t-1}$, violence behavior$_{t-1}$, violence of others, alliance committments$_{t-1}$, wheat production, coal output.

SUBJECTIVE VERSUS OBJECTIVE FORECASTING METHODS

But how are (or should) forecasting methodologies (be) selected? Typically, methods are selected on the basis of how familiar an analyst is with a particular method or methods. Often, methods are selected independent of the forecasting problem at hand, where a problem-solver will try to fit the familiar method to whatever problem appears. What are so often missing in applied forecasting are selection criteria. For example, faced with a real-time forecasting problem, such as when and where the next international crisis might occur, would/should a problem-solver select an essentially empirical method, such as pattern recognition or regression, or a Bayesian one? Indeed, both methods are viable, but why one and not the other, or why not both? What does one gain (or lose) from the use of one instead of the other? How much better would a *combined* forecast be?

Clearly, costs must be related to multiple criteria which should be applied to the forecasting problem. Marvin Cetron and Charles Ralph in their *Industrial Applications of Technological Forecasting* (New York: Wiley-Interscience, 1971), have suggested six:

+ Amount of Time Necessary to Prepare the Forecast
+ Amount of Data Required for the Forecast
+ Degree of Reproducibility of the Forecast
+ Visibility, or Objectivity, of the Method to the Potential User
+ Confidence in the Accuracy of the Method
+ Implicit Assumptions in the Forecast

J. Scott Armstrong (*Long Range Forecasting*, New York: Wiley-Interscience, 1978) has a somewhat different list:

+ Developmental Costs
+ Maintenance Costs
+ Operating Costs
+ Uncertainty Costs
+ Learning Costs

For Armstrong, data needs, the complexity of the method, and the time and money required for implementation comprise the major factors which influence developmental costs. Maintenance costs refer to those expenses in time and effort necessary to maintain, update, and document the methods. Operating costs, unlike developmental and maintenance costs, appear no higher for complex methods. Indeed, once a complex objective method is developed, operating costs remain low because the forecasts tend to be generated by computer or by an analyst performing routine calculations. Uncertainty costs refer to the level of understatement or overstatement present in the forecast. According to Armstrong, judgmental methods are advantageous because of the different ways one can estimate uncertainty (but their major disadvantage is their tendency to understate uncertainty). Extrapolative methods offer simple and inexpensive ways to assess uncertainty and econometric methods can, in some cases, go beyond extrapolations and explain and predict the sources of uncertainty. Learning costs are more difficult to assess. Indeed, it has often been said that expertise ... breeds an inability to accept new views. Accordingly, it may be difficult to learn or teach a forecasting method which is exceedingly complex and relies upon knowledge and experience in fields unrelated to forecasting. This is obviously the case with regard to the learning and teaching of objective forecasting methodology insofar as such methodology requires at least a rudimentary knowledge of statistics and mathematics. On the other hand, the Bayesian techniques are rather easily explained and understood.

Figure 6.10 constitutes a simple forecasting method selector. It looks at required talent, time, support, cost, and data. It also suggests that if the tools necessary for the conduct of a forecast are not immediately available, then to some extent at least the choice of one's method is predetermined. The chart also fails to present any definitive ideas regarding reliability and appropriateness. This is deliberate primarily because the ultimate effectiveness of a forecasting methodology lies principally in how well it is executed. And, as the chart below suggests, a forecasting method cannot be executed effectively unless all of the tools of forecasting problem-solving are available. The questions of reliability and appropriateness are also ignored here because there presently exists tremendous inconclusive debate regarding the strengths and weaknesses of each methodology in terms of long-term reliability and appropriateness. Indeed, some analysts are absolutely convinced that the Bayesian techniques are only useful for short-range forecasting; at the same time, a great many others feel exactly the same way about regression techniques. Clearly, the techniques themselves are not necessarily inherently range, goal, or object limited. Rather, any technique—if properly understood and implemented—can yield multiple goals with reference to varied forecasting objects.

CRITERIA / METHODS	TALENT		TIME		SUPPORT		COST		DATA	
	HIGH	LOW	HIGH	LOW	HIGH	LOW	HIGH	LOW	HIGH	LOW
INTUITION		✓		✓		✓		✓		✓
DELPHI		✓	✓			✓		✓		✓
CROSS IMPACT		✓	✓			✓		✓		✓
BAYESIAN	✓		✓	✓	✓	✓	✓	✓	✓	✓
EXTRAPOLATIVE	✓		✓		✓			✓	✓	
MULTIPLE REGRESSION	✓		✓		✓		✓		✓	
ECONOMETRIC MODELING	✓		✓		✓		✓		✓	

FIGURE 6.10
FORECASTING METHOD SELECTOR

Summary

Forecasts are usually required as part of a larger analytical problem, but are sometimes required independent of any larger context. Before selecting a forecasting method, problem-solvers should specify the forecasting objects and goals. The objects of forecasting include events and conditions, and forecasting goals may be distinguished according to how far into the future they are expected to "see."

Debates about the appropriateness and reliability of forecasting methods should be settled by the requirements of specific problem-solving situations. When qualified experts are available, and the forecasting problem is unsolvable via the use of quantitative-empirical data, then subjective methods can be productively used. But on those occasions when a good deal of reliable hard data exists, and the problem is particularly suited to the use of objective methods, then such methods should be used. Subjective methods generally require less support than objective ones; objective methods also require a lot of empirical data. Fortunately, nearly all of the forecasting methods presented above have been computerized.

BIBLIOGRAPHIC ESSAY

The forecasting literature is voluminous. Every year countless books, articles, and research reports are published, reviewed, studied, and discarded. It is important to recognize the difference among these publications, however. Some are primarily concerned with developing and testing a new methodology, or, much more frequently, a new twist on an old one. Others describe a particular application of one or more methodologies. Still others devote themselves to critiquing methods and applications. Finally, too many publications propose forecasts of what the authors want to occur sometimes (and sometimes not) based upon competent analyses.

On the methodological side is Daniel Bell's "Twelve Modes of Prediction—A Preliminary Sorting of Approaches in the Social Sciences," in David V. Edwards' edited *International Political Analysis: Readings* (New York: Holt, Rinehart and Winston, 1970, pp. 378–408), which is excellent. Another excellent source is Roger K. Chisholm and Gilbert R. Whitaker's *Forecasting Methods* (Homewood, Ill: Irwin, 1971). William Sullivan and W. Wayne Claycombe's *Fundamentals of Forecasting* (Reston, VA: Reston, 1977) is especially readable and relevant to the concerns of the applied forecasters, as are J. Scott Armstrong's *Long-Range Forecasting: From Crystal Ball to Computer* (New York: Wiley-Interscience, 1978) and Steven C. Wheelwright and Spyros Makridakis' *Forecasting Methods for Management* (New York: Wiley-Interscience, 1980). Joseph P. Martino's *Technological Forecasting for Decision-Making* (New York: American Elsevier, 1972) and Vernon G. Lippitt's *Statistical Sales Forecasting* (New York: Financial Executives Research Foundation, 1969) are two good special-purpose texts. Other specific sources include Charles R. Nelson's *Applied Time Series Analysis for Managerial Forecasting* (San Francisco: Holden-Day, 1973), G.E.P. Box and G.M. Jenkins' *Time Series Analysis, Forecasting and Control* (San Francisco: Holden-Day, 1970), and Nazli Choucri's "Applications of Econometric Analysis to Forecasting in International Relations" (*Peace Research Society International Papers*, 21, 1973, pp. 15–39).

On the more applied side are Arnold Mitchell, Burnham H. Dodge, Pamela G. Kruzic, David C. Miller, Peter Schwartz, and Benjamin E. Suta's *Handbook of Forecasting Techniques* (Menlo Park, CA: Stanford Research Institute, December 1975); G. Robert Franco, Robert A. Young, James A. Moore, Mark E. Wynn, and Michael R. Leavitt's *A General Handbook for Long-Range Environmental Forecasting* (Arlington, VA: Consolidated Analysis Centers, February 1973); and Scott Barclay, Clinton W. Kelly, III, Cameron R. Peterson, Lawrence D. Phillips, and Judith Selvidge's *Handbook for Decision Analysis* (McLean, VA: Decisions and Designs, September 1977).

Some excellent subjective forecasting methodology sources include Fritz R.S. Dressler's "Subjective Methodology in Forecasting" (*Technological Forecasting and Social Change*, 3, 1972, pp. 427–439) and the large edited *Handbook of Futures Research* (Westpark, CT: Greenwood Press, 1976) by Jib Fowles. Good introductions to the use of Bayes' theorem of conditional probability and probability theory generally can be found in Barclay, et al's *Handbook for Decision Analysis*, and Frederick Mosteller, Robert E.K. Rourke, and George B. Thomas, Jr.'s *Probability: A First Course* (both published in Reading, MA: Addison-Wesley, 1970). The Delphi method can be studied in H. Sackman's *Delphi Assessment: Expert Opinion, Forecasting, and Group Process* (Santa Monica, CA: The Rand Corporation, April 1974); Norman Dalkey's *The Delphi Method: An Experimental Study of Group Opinion* (Santa Monica, CA: The Rand Corporation, June 1969); T.J. Gordon and Olaf Helmer's *Report on a Long-Range Forecasting Study* (Santa Monica, CA: The Rand Corporation, September 1964); and Kim Quaile Hill and Jib Fowles' "The Methodological Worth of the Delphi Forecasting Technique" (*Technological Forecasting and Social Change*, 7, 1975, pp. 179–192). Solid introductions to the cross-impact method can be found in many of the above general forecasting texts and in John G. Stover and Theodore J. Gordon's "Cross-Impact Analysis" in Fowles' *Handbook of Futures Research*. The complicated hierarchical inference technique is explained thoroughly and skillfully in Barclay, et al's *Handbook for Decision Analysis*.

Objective forecasting methodology is well covered in the general texts listed at the beginning of this Bibliographic Essay. Armstrong's *Long-Range Forecasting* is perhaps one of the best because it compares and contrasts a lot of objective methods.

The selection of forecasting methods is addressed in *Long-Range Forecasting*, and in M.J. Cetron and C. Ralph's *Industrial Applications of Technological Forecasting: Its Utilization in R&D Management* (New York: Wiley-Interscience, 1971).

Computer-based forecasting is discussed in Armstrong's *Long-Range Forecasting*, Stephen J. Andriole's "Computer-Based Bayesian Forecasting Methodologies", in Gerald W. Hopple and James H. Kulhman's *Expert Generated Data* (Boulder, CO: Westview Press, 1981, pp. 57–92), and Roy M. Gulick's *Documentation of Decision-Aiding Software* (McLean, VA: Decisions and Designs, September 1979). Finally, Wheelwright and Makridakis in their *Forecasting Methods for Management* discuss in some detail a powerful computerized forecasting system known as SIBYL/RUNNER. (It would also be useful to consult the Bibliographic Essay in chapter 11.)

7

Prescription

IT IS IMPORTANT to note at the outset of this chapter that the prescription of actions is the result of a set of highly interrelated steps which together comprise all decision-making processes. In fact, a great deal of research has gone into the modeling of decision processes in order to understand and improve decision-making processes. While the chapter is concerned primarily with the selection of alternatives, it is important to understand that the total decision-making process is comprised of many other tasks. Many of these tasks are addressable via the descriptive, explanatory, predictive/forecasting, and evaluation methodologies also presented in this handbook. Thus, before turning to some specific objective and subjective methods for selecting and implementing alternative actions, some solid background research which has dealt with the construction and analysis of decision process models will be presented.

DECISION PROCESS MODELS

Certainly one of the most noteworthy decision process models belongs to Harold D. Lasswell, who poses seven questions explicitly relevant to the multiple stages of the decision process in his *The Decision Process: Seven Categories of Functional Analysis* (College Park, MD: University of Maryland's Bureau of Governmental Research, 1956):

1. How is the information that comes to the attention of decision-makers gathered and processed?
2. How are recommendations made and promoted?
3. How are general rules prescribed?
4. How are the general rules provisionally invoked in reference to conduct?
5. How are general rules applied?

6. How is the working of prescriptions appraised?

7. How are the prescriptions and arrangements entered into within the framework of such rules brought to termination?

The questions themselves "refer to the seven functions" or tasks of decision-making which appear below and constitute the components of Lasswell's model:

1. Intelligence	Information, prediction, planning
2. Recommendation	Promotion of policy alternatives
3. Prescription	Enactment of general rules
4. Invocation	Provisional characterizations of conduct according to prescriptions, including demand for application
5. Application	Final characterization of conduct according to prescriptions
6. Appraisal	Assessment of the success and failure of policy
7. Termination	Ending of prescriptions and of arrangements entered into within their framework

During the *intelligence* stage, decision-makers attempt to gather as much information as their role and time perspectives allow. Following the completion of this task, decision-makers attempt to array and weight the actions or policy alternatives which they deem as feasible responses to the situation.

During the *recommendation* stage, designated policy alternatives are accepted or rejected on the basis of the "intelligence" of stage one.

Tasks three, four, and five (*prescription, invocation,* and *application*) require decision-makers to select and implement a policy alternative; during the *appraisal* stage, the activity of stages one through five are assessed; and the task of *termination* requires decision-makers to shut down the decision machinery.

Obviously, decision-makers seldom—if ever—make decisions on the basis of such a rigid rule structure. Lasswell's categories, much like those presented below, are proferred not as representations of reality, but as tools through which we might gain insight into the decision process. At the same time, the distinctions to which the models alert us enable us to understand the processes which invariably—yet only implicitly or unconsciously—occur during every decision situation. In other words, while no one individual or agency ever decided to accomplish the "intelligence" task and so on down the list, they must at some point in time think about what their problem is and from where they might get information to solve it. Decision process models enable us to lend order to and examine the process with a minimal amount of unknown distortion.

William D. Coplin has also constructed a model of the decision process. He lists four steps in his *Introduction to International Politics* (Chicago: Rand McNally, 1964) which he believes all decision-makers must execute:

1. Define the Situation
2. Select Goals
3. Search for Alternatives
4. Choose Alternatives

Charles F. Hermann also summarizes the decision-making process in his "The Knowledge Gap," presented at the annual meeting of the American Political Science Association in Chicago in September 1971:

1. Problem-Task Recognition
2. Problem and Option Definition
3. Advocacy of Options
4. Implementation
5. Evaluation

The above models represent rather idyllic and compartmentalized visions of the decision-making process. Seldom is the process unencumbered or idyllic; it is nearly always characterized by uncertainty and confusion.

Lasswell, Coplin, and Hermann all list a recognition task. Before a problem can be dealt with via the making of a "good" decision, it must be understood. But understanding is a *cognitive* phenomenon dependent upon perception and conceptualization, and influenced by personality traits, past experiences, and one's immediate environment. If problems (and opportunities) are not understood (perceived and conceptualized accurately), it is difficult to make informed decisions. In fact, many analysts, when addressing the issues related directly to perception, characterize all perception as "unreliable" and as a potentially dangerous basis for action. Obviously, the making of "inferences" does not foster the extraction of reliable perceptions and the construction of completely accurate conceptualizations.

While the problems associated with individual perception and conceptualization are certainly real, since the making of many public and private decisions is essentially a group phenomenon, they are necessarily encountered and *compounded* within a group setting. Indeed, inter-personal relationships may also breed misperception and inaccurate conceptualization. In addition, there are complexities within the decision-making process which arise as a result of the individual personalities involved. Put quite simply, since different persons have different beliefs, they will have different perceptions of the same event, and even the same people.

As if there were not enough obstacles to accurate perception and conceptualization, the "bureaucratic" threat must also be considered. While it is true that perceptions and conceptualizations are actually made by individuals within or which comprise a bureaucratic organization, it is also true that bureaucratic organizations enjoy lives of their own. Within such organizations, institutional mechanisms often prevent important facts from reaching decision-makers. Perception and conceptualization are thus often adversely affected.

Also relevant to the tasks of perception and conceptualization are the *images* which decision-makers and agencies have of themselves, their peers, and virtually every entity and experience with which they come into contact. Unlike perception, which is an internal (psychological) characterization of an *existing* or *impending* phenomenon, an image should be regarded as that which exerts an impact at all times.

In order for decision-makers to conceptualize accurately an event or condition, they must thus first do battle with the perceptions of their own psyches as well as those of their peers and agency. In addition, they must confront the images of the entire psychological and operational milieux. Only when such perceptions and images accurately mirror reality can decision-makers reliably conceptualize the dimensions of existing or impending opportunities or problems.

Based upon the above, it is easy to conceive of decision-making as all encompassing. In principle it is, although it may be conducted by many different problem-solvers at different times and places. In practice, then, individual problem-solvers are generally responsible for but one aspect of the decision-making process with or without knowledge of the other aspects. This chapter is concerned exclusively with the selection of alternative actions, options, and/or decisions.

METHODS

Prescriptive methods, like predictive-forecasting methods, may be distinguished according to how subjective or objective they are. Subjective prescriptive methods are those which rely upon the judgments of decision-makers, while objective ones rely upon the manipulation of quantitative-empirical data. Again, this handbook will not decide which general method is the best; the parameters of the specific prescriptive problem-solving situation should determine which methods are selected and rejected.

SUBJECTIVE METHODS

The useful subjective methods can be differentiated according to whether or not they assume uncertainty in the option selection process. For example, some methods permit decision-makers to select a specific option without regard to any uncertain events or conditions that might exert an impact upon the selection process. Other methods enable decision-makers to deal with uncertainty in a manner which permits them to maximize the value connected with individual options.

Option Selection Under Conditions of Relative Certainty

Imagine a scenario where you have decided to purchase a new car. You have the money, and cars are available, so there is no uncertainty connected with the decision. But you have looked at and test-driven no less than seven cars and cannot make up your mind.

The first step toward a quick selection involves making a list of the factors (or selection criteria) important to your choice. They might very well include cost, gas mileage, comfort, appearance, and overall quality of construction. The next step is to define these criteria so they will be consistently used when you perform the next step, scoring (on a scale of 1 to 10), as suggested in Figure 7.1.

The scoring itself can be done in absolute terms, quickly, and extremely easily, as Figure 7.1 suggests. Note also that car #1, with a score of 31 is the winner and car #4 a close runner-up with a score of 30. But note that #1 is extremely expensive and that #4 is extremely inexpensive. One variation to the process, then, might involve weighting the criteria in terms of their overall importance to the decision. In the new car selection example, if cost were heavily weighted in terms of importance, then car #1 could not possible "win."

Criteria / Cars	# 1	# 2	# 3	# 4	# 5	# 6	# 7
COST	1	6	4	9	2	7	3
GAS MILEAGE	9	7	4	5	2	1	1
COMFORT	8	4	6	4	7	3	1
APPEARANCE	7	8	4	6	5	7	2
QUALITY	6	2	7	6	6	6	4
TOTAL	31	27	25	30	22	24	11

FIGURE 7.1
QUICK (UNWEIGHTED) NEW CAR SELECTION

The steps necessary to conduct a *weighted* attribute analysis, as suggested in Percy Hill, et. al's *Making Decisions* (Reading, MA: Addison-Wesley, 1980), are as follows:

1. Identify decision alternatives.

2. Define decision alternatives.

3. Identify evaluation selection criteria.

4. Define evaluation selection criteria.

5. Rank the criteria according to their relative importance.

6. Determine criteria weighting factors according to the formula below:

Evaluative Criteria	Rank/ Points	Weighting Factors
Cost	1/5	5/15 = 0.33+
Mileage	2/4	4/15 = 0.26+
Appearance	3/3	3/15 = 0.20+
Quality	4/2	2/15 = 0.13+
Comfort	5/1	1/15 = 0.06+
	15	15/15 = 1.0

7. Develop a decision matrix, as suggested in Figure 7.2.

8. Score the alternatives against the criteria, one criteria at a time, on a 10-to-1 (highest-to-lowest) scale.

9. Multiply the scores X the weighting factors.

10. Select the alternative with the highest total/weighted score, as suggested in Figure 7.3.

The above unweighted and weighted decision option selection methods are useful when the alternatives are relatively few in number (ten or less), when the criteria are few and one dimensional, and when speed is required. But they are not the most diagnostic methods available.

Another "multi-attribute utility" evaluation method formalizes and extends the above procedures. Developed by Ward Edwards in his "How to Use Multi-Attri-

Criteria / Weighting Factors / Cars		# 1	# 2	# 3	# 4	# 5	# 6	# 7
Cost	0.33							
Gas Mileage	0.26							
Appearance	0.20							
Quality	0.13							
Comfort	0.06							
TOTAL	1.00							

FIGURE 7.2
WEIGHTED SELECTION MATRIX

Weighting Factors / Criteria	Cars	#1	#2	#3	#4	#5	#6	#7
Cost	0.33	1 / 0.33	6 / 1.98	4 / 1.32	9 / 2.97	2 / 0.66	7 / 2.31	3 / 0.99
Gas Mileage	0.26	9 / 2.34	7 / 1.82	4 / 1.04	5 / 1.30	2 / 0.52	1 / 0.26	1 / 0.26
Appearance	0.20	7 / 1.40	8 / 1.60	4 / 0.80	6 / 1.20	5 / 1.00	7 / 1.40	2 / 0.40
Quality	0.13	6 / 0.78	2 / 0.26	7 / 0.91	6 / 0.78	6 / 0.78	6 / 0.78	4 / 0.52
Comfort	0.06	8 / 0.48	4 / 0.24	6 / 0.36	4 / 0.24	7 / 0.42	3 / 0.18	1 / 0.06
TOTAL	1.00	5.33	5.90	4.43	6.49	3.18	4.93	2.24

FIGURE 7.3
WEIGHTED NEW CAR SELECTION

bute Utility Measurement for Social Decisionmaking" (*IEEE Transactions on Systems, Man, and Cybernetics*, 7, May 1977, pp. 326–40), the method also requires ten steps:

1. Identify the person(s) or organizations whose values are to be maximized.

2. Identify the issue or issues (i.e., decisions) to which the values are needed.

3. Identify the choices to be considered.

4. Identify the relevant dimensions of value, or criteria, for consideration.

5. Rank the criteria in order of importance.

6. Rate the criteria in importance, preserving ratios by assigning the least important criteria an importance of 10. Then consider the next least important criteria. How much more important is it than the least important? Assign it a number that reflects this ratio. Repeat for all of the criteria.

7. Sum the importance weights, and divide each by the sum. This step converts importance weights into numbers that are mathematically close to probabilities.

8. Measure the location of each entity being evaluated on each criterion by estimating the position of the entity on that criterion on a 0–100 scale, where 0 is minimum and 100 is maximum value.

9. Calculate the values for the entities being considered. The equation is:

$$V_i = \Sigma_j w_j V_{ij}$$

remembering that $\Sigma_j w_j = 1$. V_i is the aggregate value (or utility) for the *i*th entity. w_j is the normalized importance weight of the *j*th dimension of value, and V_{ij} is the rescaled position of the *i*th entity on the *j*th dimension.

10. Decide by a simple rule: maximize V_i.

The multi-attribute utility methodology described above has been computerized in a computer program known as EVAL. Developed by Decisions and Designs, Inc., EVAL permits a user to identify options, name criteria, weight criteria, and score the options interactively at a mini- or microcomputer terminal. But unlike the above relatively simple techniques, EVAL enables a user to decompose the evaluative criteria to their simplest (yet still diagnostic) levels, as suggested in Figure 7.4. This de-

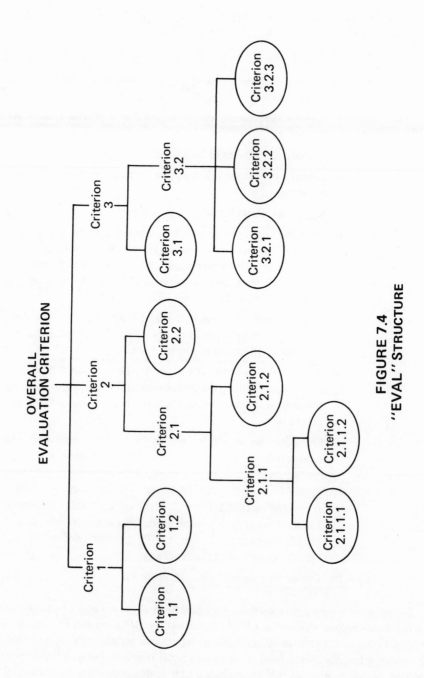

FIGURE 7.4
"EVAL" STRUCTURE

composition capability facilitates extremely thorough decision option evaluations in a rapid and flexible manner: EVAL also permits on-line sensitivity analyses where the user can vary the criteria weights and decision option scores to determine what impact the variance might have upon the selection of the most "worthy" option (see the Bibliographic Essay and chapter 8 for more information about EVAL).

All of these techniques for option selection under conditions of relative uncertainty are straightforward and versatile enough to be used to select among all kinds of decision options. However, excessive complexity is the common enemy of them all. They are not designed to be used to select among an unlimited number of alternatives or to evaluate alternatives against an unlimited number of criteria. A great deal of front-end work is thus required to make sure that the application does not get bogged down in unnecessary detail. It is especially important to avoid redundant evaluative criteria, and criteria which are only marginally important to the decision problem. Finally, it is absolutely critical to apply these techniques as honestly as possible, because it is possible to manipulate the process by predetermining the desired outcome.

Option Selection Under Conditions of Relative Uncertainty

Classic decision trees can be used productively by decision makers to select options when there is one or more key uncertainty tied to the decision problem. For example, imagine a situation which requires a decision regarding whether or not to invest in one company or another. The required investment in Company A is $100,-000, while $90,000 is required for Company B. The expected return on the investment in Company A is $400,000; $500,000 is expected from Company B. But the likelihood of realizing the money depends upon whether or not the companies succeed or fail in their respective businesses. Assuming that the probability of success and failure for Company A is 0.4 and 0.6, respectively, and that the success/failure probability of Company B is 0.6 and 0.4, respectively, in order to calculate the expected value of investing in Company A and B given the probabilities of success and failure, the decision-maker must simply multiply the probability times the estimated payoff and add the results, all as suggested in Figure 7.5.

This is obviously an extremely simple example. Not only was there only one key uncertainty but "value" was defined unidimensionally. Nearly all decision problems require the development of more complicated decision trees. (In fact, since decision trees can grow to enormous sizes, computer support is highly desirable.) Another important variation is the conversion of "value" into standard "utiles," that is, into non-monetary units. This conversion enables decision-makers to deal easily with complex, multi-attributed decision outcome values.

Finally, it must be emphasized that decision trees do not make decisions. Nor do they suggest exactly how a decision-maker should behave. Instead, they describe in a standard way the likely payoffs given certain event probabilities. Ultimately, the option implemented will reflect the decision-maker's attitudes toward risk as much as it represents the greatest expected value.

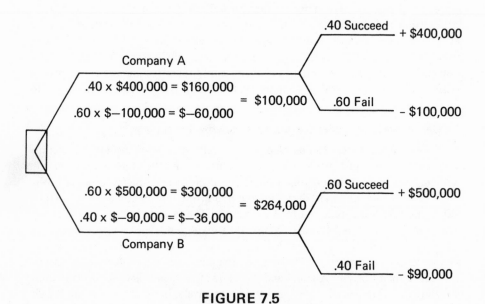

FIGURE 7.5
SIMPLE DECISION TREE

Group Decision-Making

As suggested in the beginning of this chapter, prescription is frequently encumbered by the perceptions, images, biases and attitudes of individual decision-makers as well as by the compounded effects of group interaction. Unfortunately, the number of problem-solving difficulties tends to rise exponentially as the number of problem-solvers rises. Disagreements often arise regarding even agendas. Decision-makers who find themselves members of a decision-making group should thus take special precautions to avoid discussions and arguments which have little to do with solving the decision problem.

One way to deal with group decision-making problems is to conduct a Delphi decision analysis where the participants decide about values and probabilities anonymously. This can be accomplished via the development and use of paper questionnaires and decision trees, or with the aid of a computer-based group decision-making system.

Developed by Perceptronics, Inc., the computer-based group decision aid allows members of a group to input their respective estimates regarding the occurrence of specific events as well as their values regarding the importance of specific decision outcomes. The computer-based group decision aid aggregates such input and then informs the group members about disagreements among them. Finally, it suggests to the group precisely how their agreements might be resolved. Most importantly, it informs them about those dimensions of the decision which are relatively unimportant vis-a-vis the group's decision-making goal and simultaneously focuses discussion upon disagreements among members of the group which are important toward realizing the group's postulated goal. The group aid functions as follows and as illustrated in Figure 7.6:

- ◆ The decision-making group is composed of the participants, an intermediator, and a director. The participants are the decision-makers. The intermediator and the director are procedural interfaces between the participants and the computer.

- ◆ The intermediator takes the participant's requests and formats them for input to the decision aid. The inputs are lists of alternative actions and events, modifications to previously stored information, and commands for the display of selected information.

- ◆ The director is an interface in the other direction, taking the computer's output (often instructions as to what to do next) and presenting them to the participants.

- ◆ The group director focuses the group's activities and ensures that the group's inputs are appropriate for the decision aid.

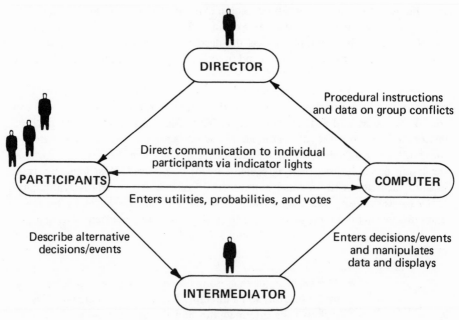

FIGURE 7.6
COMPUTER-BASED GROUP DECISION AID

The Bayesian group decision aid enables groups to move much more swiftly toward decisions and also generates data useful for "profiling" decision-makers. This by-product enables managers to compile lists of decision-makers with expertise in specific areas. They also know which decision-makers tend to be risk averse or risk takers. Indeed, after enough group decision experiences, a manager should know precisely who to call (and who to avoid) to solve particular decision problems.

OBJECTIVE METHODS

As with predictive methodology, the distinction between objective and subjective methodology can be seen in the origins and treatment of data. Objective action selection methods thus often rely upon empirical-statistical manipulations of the information relevant to the selection of one decision option or another. For example, values can be empirically determined and correlated against outcome variables in order to determine the attractiveness of a particular option. Instead of subjectively determined values, empirically derived ones can be generated. Relationships among them can also be empirically determined. Problem-solvers can also predict via regression analyses the values of particular variables over time. While subjective methods require little empirical data, the more objective ones require a great deal. They also usually require computer support.

Option Selection Via Statistical Association

An excellent example of a quantitative-empirical option selection tool was developed by CACI, Inc. for the U.S. Department of Defense. The idea involved an analysis of past actions taken by the U.S. during crisis situations and a determination regarding how effective the actions were. From this analysis a data base was constructed which enabled decision-makers to determine which action would be most likely to succeed given a particular decision-making requirement. Figure 7.7 suggests how this prototype system can generate output regarding what action(s) to take given a requirement to regain access to economic resources. The figure also suggests which of the actions is most likely to succeed. The vertical lines in the figure suggest the strength of the association between the actions and the postulated goal.

Obviously one cannot generate reliable associations between decision options and goals unless there are a great many cases to associate or correlate (see chapters 4 and 5). Caution must also guide the use of such associations because by definition statistical associations capture broad patterns in the data; they never isolate irregular nuances. Consequently, methods based upon statistical association and/or correlation must be carefully implemented. (Incidently, the crisis management decision aid described above has yet to generate any real enthusiasm in the Department of Defense.)

Option Selection Via Linear, Nonlinear, and Causal Modeling

Some decision problems can be solved with large amounts of quantitative-empirical data and models geared to generate output which can be fed directly into

REGAIN ACCESS TO ECONOMIC RESOURCES

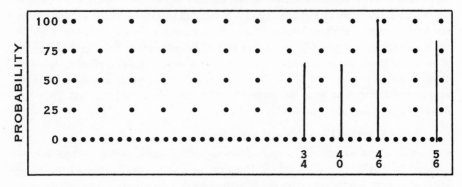

**CONDITIONAL PROBABILITIES OF
ASSOCIATED U.S. ACTIONS**

U.S. ACTIONS

34 **PROVIDE SUPPLIES FROM NON-MILITARY SOURCES**
40 **ACCEPT A NEW MILITARY COST**
46 **EMPLOY DIPLOMACY**
56 **U.S. ACTS WITH TWO OR MORE OTHER NATIONS**

FIGURE 7.7
STATISTICALLY ASSOCIATED OPTION SELECTION

a decision-making process. For example, it is possible to develop a series of multiple regression equations to predict the values of certain variables and then plug those values into a decision tree. Similarly, decision outcome values can be calculated and used to determine multi-attribute values. Linear, nonlinear, and causal models can be used to generate such input; however, as always it is important to remember that large amounts of data are necessary to activate these models and that sometimes the effort required to develop and apply such models may be disproportionate to the decision problem at hand.

SUBJECTIVE VERSUS OBJECTIVE PRESCRIPTIVE METHODS

The costs and benefits of subjective and objective prescriptive methods are hard to assess because personal preference, experience, availability, and so forth all play a part in the assessment. Generally, however, the decision analytic and multi-attribute utility methods can be applied relatively easier than their objective counterparts. The selection of one or another method should also be made in conjunction with general problem-solving tools assessments.

Overall, the option selection methods can be implemented under conditions of relative certainty much easier than under conditions of relative uncertainty. If possible, then, try to minimize uncertainty before the option selection process begins. Also, make sure there is enough time to list and scrutinize as many decision alternatives as possible. Computer support for option selection problems under conditions of relative certainty is not absolutely necessary, although the computer program EVAL can accelerate the option evaluation process. Decisions made under conditions of relative uncertainty via the development of decision trees can be extremely time consuming and complicated. Here computer support is almost essential. Decision tree construction also requires a great deal of patience and an appreciation for detail. In short, if you or your decision-making group is by nature impatient, then either avoid decision trees or establish two decision-making groups, one to deal with the uncertainty and one to deal with the values of decision outcomes. After these groups have had a chance to work on their respective problems a session can be convened to integrate the probability and value estimates into a decision tree.

Group decision processes are especially tricky. Not only must a number of very different professionals work together effectively but every effort must be made to minimize the effect of inhibiting adminstrative and bureaucratic processes. The sociological realities of group problem-solving are also potentially threatening to efficient option selection. Anonymous probability and value estimation should be considered when the decision-making group is comprised of a lot of strong-willed problem-solvers of many ranks. The computer-based group decision aid can accelerate group problem-solving as can any system which preserves anonymity and accelerates an otherwise very tedious process.

Objective methods should be used to inform the option selection process when the problem area is clear. For example, sales forecasts based upon ten years of hard data can be used to decide upon how much money to invest in plant expansion. Monetary values can also be determined from past experience and then used to evaluate options or build decision trees. But unless the data is diagnostic, the use of objective prescriptive methods will not be worthwhile. Computer support is also necessary to implement the methods as is considerable human support. All of the objective and subjective methods require a good deal of expertise, except perhaps those which involve selecting options under conditions of relative certainty.

SUMMARY

All decision-making requires the execution of a number of sequential steps which always involve at a minimum the formulation of goals, the identification of alternatives, the gathering of information, and the evaluation of alternatives. Subjective methods include the assigning of numeric values to decision alternatives, the weighting of criteria to evaluate decision alternatives, the integration of event probabilities which will impact upon the selection of alternatives, the conduct of anonymous group decision-making, and the computerization of all of the above. The objective methods include option selection via the use of association, correlation, and regression. Subjective methods are easier to implement than objective ones because data, support, and expertise requirements are relatively high. At the same time, the development and use of decision trees is also very time and labor intensive.

BIBLIOGRAPHIC ESSAY

Decision option selection and alternative evaluation is complex. While there are relatively simple techniques available, they all presume logic and consistency on the part of the user. The subjective techniques are by and large related to what is known broadly as decision analysis. It is important to note, however, that this handbook does not in any way constitute a blueprint for the full application potential of decision analysis. Creative users of the technology will no doubt expand use into realms left undiscussed here. Rex V. Brown, Andrew S. Kahr, and Cameron R. Peterson's *Decision Analysis for the Manager* (New York: Holt, Rinehart and Winston, 1974) is a very good semi-applied text as is the *Handbook for Decision Analysis*, a government-funded report written by Scott Barclay, Rex V. Brown, Clinton W. Kelly, III, Cameron R. Peterson, Lawrence D. Phillips, and Judith Selvidge (McLean, VA: Decisions and Designs, September 1977). The Barclay et al *Handbook* is an extremely good introduction to subjective information processing. Dennis Lindley's *Making Decisions* (New York: John Wiley, 1973); Howard Raiffa's *Decision Analysis: Analysis of Decisions Under Uncertainty* (New York: Addison-Wesley, 1968); Ward Edwards' excellent "How to Use Multi-Attribute Utility Measurement for Social Decisionmaking" (*IEEE Transactions on Systems, Man, and Cybernetics*, 7, May 1977, pp. 326–40); and Percy Hill et al's *Making Decisions* (Reading, MA: Addison-Wesley, 1980) are all also very relevant to understanding subjective methodology. Stephen

J. Andriole's "Decision Process Models and the Needs of Policy-Makers" (*Policy Sciences*, 11, December 1979, pp. 19–37) and Y. Chou's *Probability and Statistics for Decision-Making* (New York: Holt, Rinehart and Winston, 1972) are also useful. On the objective side are R.V. Hartley's *Operations Research: A Managerial Emphasis* (Pacific Palisades, CA: Goodyear, 1976); Richard E. Trueman's *Quantitative Methods for Decision Making* (New York: Holt, Rinehart and Winston, 1977); R.E. Willis and N.L. Chervany's *Statistical Analysis and Modeling for Management Decision Making* (Belmont, CA: Wadsworth, 1974); and H.B. Wagner's *Principles of Operations with Applications to Managerial Decisions* (Englewood Cliffs, N.J.: Prentice-Hall, 1975). For those interested in the theoretical bases of decision analysis and decision-making, the journal *Decision Sciences* is a good source. Information on the Perceptronics, Inc. group decision aid can be found in Steven Levin, Antonio Leal, and Joseph Saleh's *An Interactive Computer Aiding System for Group Decision-Making* (Rosslyn, VA: Perceptronics, June 1977). Information about the crisis management executive aid can be found in Leo A. Hazlewood and John J. Hayes' *Planning for Problems in Crisis Management* (Rosslyn, VA: CACI, September 1976). EVAL and several other pieces of decision option selection computer software funded by the U.S. federal government are discussed in Linda B. Allardyce, Dorothy M. Amey, Phillip H. Feuerwerger, and Roy M. Gulick's *Documentation of Decision-Aiding Software: DECISION Functional Description* (McLean, VA: Decisions and Designs, September 1979); Linda B. Allardyce, Dorothy M. Amey, Phillip H. Feuerwerger, and Roy M. Gulick's *Documentation of Decision Aiding Software: DECISION Users Manual* (McLean, VA: Decisions and Designs, September 1979); Linda B. Allardyce, Dorothy M. Amey, Phillip H. Feuerwerger, and Roy M. Gulick's *Documentation of Decision-Aiding Software: EVAL Functional Description* (McLean, VA: Decisions and Designs, September 1979); and Linda B. Allardyce, Dorothy M. Amey, Phillip H. Feuerwerger, and Roy M. Gulick's *Documentation of Decision Aiding Software: EVAL Users Manual* (McLean, VA: Decisions and Designs, September 1979).

Background literature on the decision-making process can be found in Harold D. Lasswell's *The Decision Process: Seven Categories of Functional Analysis* (College Park, MD: University of Maryland's Bureau of Governmental Research, 1956); James E. Anderson's *Public Policy-Making* (New York: Praeger, 1975); William D. Coplin's *Introduction to International Politics* (Chicago: Rand McNally, 1964); and Charles F. Hermann's "The Knowledge Gap: The Exchange of Information Between the Academic and Foreign Policy Communities," presented at the Annual Meeting of the American Political Science Association, Chicago, Illinois, September 7–11, 1971. Also of background interest is Jerome Kagan and Ernest Havemann's *Psychology: An Introduction* (New York: Harcourt, Brace, and World, 1968), where one can find a good discussion of the processes of cognitive perception and images.

8

Evaluation

FREQUENTLY problem-solvers are asked to evaluate: analysts are often asked to evaluate systems, decision options, software, and programs, and managers are expected to evaluate personnel and administrative procedures. Yet a major distinction among evaluation problems often goes undrawn; the selection of appropriate methodologies is thus frequently misguided. Succinctly, the distinction has to do with the evaluation of processes versus entities. This distinction, and several others, is discussed below.

EVALUABILITY ASSESSMENT

Before an evaluation problem is tackled, problem-solvers should spend a specific amount of time assessing just how amenable to evaluation that which he or she is supposed to evaluate really is. As a general rule, if one cannot identify, define, or otherwise scope an evaluation object, then it cannot be evaluated. Also, an evaluation problem which is essentially subjective (in nature and content, not treatment) is probably unaddressable; that is, if the evaluation object is of a fundamentally arbitrary essence (as would be the case regarding music, some design questions, and the "attractiveness" of a particular piece of computer hardware), then an evaluation analysis would be pointless.

All of this falls under the heading of *evaluability assessment*, which requires a problem-solver to organize and define all of the components of an evaluation problem before proceeding, and, before proceeding, making sure that the components are treatable. If they are found to be beyond the range of evaluation methodology and goals, then the analysis should not take place.

In addition, evaluability assessments should determine if the evaluation is to be of a process or an entity. Process evaluation involves the analysis of phenomena such as systems, programs, models, administrative procedures, policies, and research projects. Among these, programs and policies are the best examples and the most thoroughly studied.

131

Joseph S. Wholey suggests that evaluability assessments of process problems contain the following steps ("Evaluability Assessment," in Leonard Rutman's edited *Evaluation Research Methods*, Beverly Hills, CA: Sage Publications, 1977):

1. Bounding the problem: determining what activities and what objectives constitute the process—what is the process that is to be analyzed?

2. Collection of process information: gathering information that defines process objectives, activities, and underlying assumptions.

3. Modeling: development of a model that describes the process and the interrelationships of activities and objectives, from the point of view of the intended user of the evaluation information.

4. Analysis: determining to what extent the process definition, as represented by the model, is sufficiently unambiguous that evaluation is likely to be useful.

5. Presentation to management/intended user: feedback of the results of the assessment to representatives of management/intended user and determination of next steps that should be taken.

Following this assessment, a process evaluation study can be organized and planned. The first step is to determine explicitly the goals and purpose(s) of the evaluation. Leonard Rutman, in his "Planning an Evaluation Study" (in Rutman's *Evaluation Research Methods*), suggests that problem-solvers look for covert and overt purposes. Covert purposes include the following:

♦ "Eyewash"—A deliberate focus on the superficial to make a process or entity look good.

♦ "Whitewash"—An attempt to cover up process failures.

♦ "Submarine"—The political use of research for destructive purposes.

♦ "Posture"—Evaluation research as a ritual having little substance (often undertaken only because it was a condition for funding).

♦ "Postponement"—Using evaluation to postpone needed action.

Problem-solvers should also determine who initiated an evaluation and why, and be prepared to answer questions about how he or she plans to conduct the evaluation and why. Overt purposes are usually much more easily discovered.

Process evaluations can focus upon the process as a whole, inputs to the process, process outcomes, and/or internal processes.

In addition to process evaluations are those which focus primarily upon a specific objective, person, product, and/or service. Such evaluations are explicitly geared to the value or worth of a particular non-process usually determined by means of criteria and/or indicators. Examples of this kind include evaluations of specific personnel, decisions, policy outcomes, automobiles, and data. The essence of entity evaluation lies in its concentration upon goals, outcomes, performance, and end-states rather than upon processes.

The steps connected with entity evaluation are similar to those connected with process evaluation except nearly all of the effort is concentrated upon identifying and developing measures of value or worth against which the entity can be evaluated.

METHODS

Evaluation methodology, perhaps unlike predictive and prescriptive methodology, has evolved along with the areas which have most required its development. For example, public policy program evaluation methodology is quite well developed but less than adequately applied to other than program evaluation problems. Nevertheless, the basic epistemological distinction between subjective and objective methodology can be used to identify some available evaluation methodologies.

SUBJECTIVE METHODS

Subjective *process* evaluative methods can involve the use of surveys, questionnaires, and judgments to capture opinions about how well (or badly) a process or subprocess is doing. Ad hoc working groups can also be established. Simulations of ideal processes can also be conducted and then compared with the actual process under evaluation.

Basically, subjective process evaluation involves the use of experts. However, since in any evaluation many people will have vested interests in the results, great care should be taken during the evaluability assessment stage to avoid selecting experts with axes to grind.

Subjective *entity* evaluation methodology, by far the most preferred kind of evaluation methodology, has been developed to the point where it can be quickly and easily implemented on a microcomputer. Based upon Ward Edwards' multi-attribute utility (MAU) theory (see chapter 7), and recently under U.S. government support, Decisions and Designs, Inc. developed EVAL.

EVAL is an evaluation methodology software system. Its general purpose is to aid problem-solvers by providing them a capability to construct, store, retrieve, exercise, and solve complex evaluation problems.

A MAU model is hierarchical, starting with the overall top-level criterion for which a comparative evaluation is desired. It is then decomposed into its component criteria in descending levels of the hierarchy such that each lower-level criterion is more specific than the ones at the preceeding level.

The fundamental product of EVAL is a MAU assessment model, as presented in Figure 8.1.

Each MAU model is constructed by using the same hierarchical format, which always consists of the following elements (or steps):

- ◆ Evaluation Problem
- ◆ Evaluative Criteria
- ◆ Alternative Entities
- ◆ Utility Scores
- ◆ Criteria Importance Weights

The input specifications describing the model can produce the following results:

Overall Results—The overall value or worth associated with each alternative. For each alternative, the overall utility is obtained by weighting and adding the utility scores assigned to the bottom-level criteria and continuing to aggregate from bottom to top. Scores for any specified higher-level criterion are calculated and displayed in the same manner.

Normalized Weights—A set of vectors corresponding to the relative importance weights of the criteria. A set of relative importance weights is assigned to the criteria comprising any specific higher-level factor. These weights are normalized into percentages by dividing each assigned weight by the sum of the weights of the component criteria.

Intermediate Results—A set of utilities assigned to any of the intermediate criteria during the calculation of the overall result.

Cumulative Weights—A set of weights corresponding to the relative importance weights of the criteria. These are calculated as follows: the top-level criteria comprising the overall evaluation have cumulative weights equal to their normalized weights. At the next lower level, the criteria are assigned a cumulative weight computed by multiplying the normalized weight by the cumulative weight of the factor to which it is attached, and dividing the product by 100. This process is continued down through the structure until all criteria have been assigned cumulative weights. The cumulative weight indicates the relative importance of the criterion to the overall evaluation.

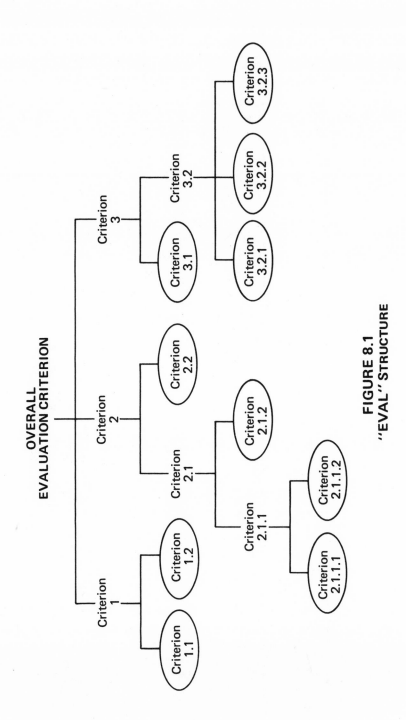

FIGURE 8.1
"EVAL" STRUCTURE

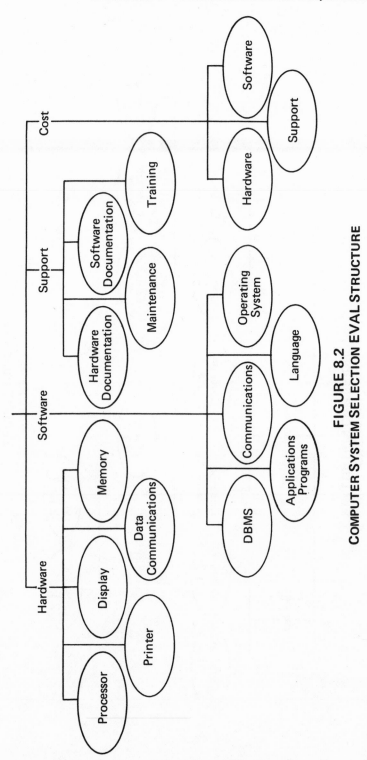

FIGURE 8.2
COMPUTER SYSTEM SELECTION EVAL STRUCTURE

As should be clear, multi-attribute utility-based evaluation can be used to assess the value of alternative decisions and any other entity for which evaluative criteria can be developed. MAU methodology is thus a prescriptive and evaluative methodology. Figure 8.2 combines a decision/entity alternative evaluation pertaining to a decision regarding which computer system to purchase. In order to make the MAU structure or model in Figure 8.2 "perform," the criteria would have to be weighted and then the various computer systems would have to be scored (evaluated) against the weighted criteria.

OBJECTIVE METHODS

Objective *process* evaluation methods are as varied as the statistical methods available to identify and measure relationships among the variables which become part of the evaluation model. Such variables may be restricted to inputs to the process under investigation or all-inclusive. In program evaluation, for example, relationships are posited to exit; the evaluation then confirms or denies the hypotheses.

Data about the components can be collected in a variety of ways and analyzed to determine how a process "works," how well it performs (against a set of performance measures), what parts are not working, what parts are working, and what parts are superfluous.

Objective *entity* evaluation is identical to subjective entity evaluation in every sense except the way the data are processed to score how well (or badly) the entities "perform." For example, and assuming that quantitative-empirical data is available and that valid measures of worth can be constructed, one can easily imagine a pure objective evaluation of several automobiles against criteria such as gas mileage, wheelbase, cost, available options, trunk space, interior space, and acceleration. Since all of these criteria are empirically measurable, and since the necessary empirical data is available, objective entities' evaluation (of automobiles, in this case) is quite possible. However, as soon as one adds criteria such as attractiveness and comfort, more subjective methods should be employed.

Objective entity analysis, then, involves goal and/or performance specifications, criteria and/or indicator development, and analysis. The results are the product of empirical data processed in quantitative ways.

RESOURCE ALLOCATION

A special kind of evaluation problem involves the allocation of resources, be they monetary, human, or material. Frequently, problem-solvers must evaluate costs and benefits in order to determine optimal allocation strategies.

Cost-Benefit Allocation Methods

Cost-benefit (or benefit-cost) analyses are most appropriately conducted when the costs can be estimated in clearcut quantitative terms and when benefits can be quantified (subjectively and objectively) in a similar manner. If the dimensions of value are too complex or numerous, then it will be difficult to conduct a useful cost-benefit analysis. Costs must also be relatively easy to determine. For example, the evaluation of alternative plant sites would be an appropriate cost-benefit problem, but the hiring of elementary school teachers would be much more difficult to evaluate.

In his "Benefit Cost Evaluation" (in Rutman's *Evaluation Research Methods*), M. Andrieu lists the following steps for the conduct of a cost-benefit analysis:

- ◆ Definition of Objectives
- ◆ Identification of Alternatives
- ◆ Listing of Costs
- ◆ Listing of Benefits
- ◆ Quantification of Costs and Benefits
- ◆ Calculation
- ◆ Listing of Assumptions
- ◆ Interpretation of Results and Recommendations

In a carefully selected and organized cost-benefit analysis, costs are more easily determined than benefits, which frequently must be determined by developing benefit indices and/or indicators. One must also guard against the designation of too many dimensions of benefit and pay very special attention to the quantification of both costs and benefits.

The calculation of costs and benefits can be accomplished in a number of ways. Usually, in order to make costs and benefits comparable, a "discount rate" is developed. Discount rates enable present values for future costs and benefits to be established. For example, $5,000 today is unlikely to be worth $5,000 in two years. Indeed, at 10% interest, $5,000 will be worth $6,050 in two years (independent, of course, of inflation). On the other hand, however, $5,000 in two years with no interest will be worth $4,133 today (or $4,133 X 10% X 2 years = $5,000). Clearly, then $5,000 today is worth more than $5,000 in two years.

The same discount rate must be applied throughout the cost-benefit process regardless of which specific method of cost-benefit calculation is used. Three of these methods are the most frequently used. They include, again after Andrieu, the following:

> *Present Value/Net Benefits Method*—the calculation of benefits minus costs (net benefits) discounted to the present.

Benefit-Cost Ratio Method—The calculation of efficiency arrived at by dividing discounted benefits by costs, which produces a per dollar efficiency figure for each (program, project, and so forth) alternative.

Rate-of-Return Method—The calculation of the discount rate to equate cost/benefit present values (based upon the assumption that the higher the benefit/cost ratio, the higher the rate of return must be to equate discounted benefits of costs).

Costs and benefits can be determined objectively, but are usually determined subjectively. Arguments frequently arise when benefits are quantified subjectively, however. The process of cost/benefit quantification/calculation can also be very time consuming and data intensive. In response to these and other problems, Decisions and Designs, Inc. has, with some U.S. government funding, developed a cost/benefit resource allocation software system called RAM (for *r*esource *a*llocation *m*odeling). RAM is a model-building system that supports the process of allocating monetary resources among competing alternatives. Its general purpose is to aid problem-solvers by giving them the capability to construct, store, and refine cost/benefit models. The overall objective of RAM is to prioritize the allocation of resources in a manner that is logically consistent with the problem-solvers' *subjective* value structure.

The RAM model assumes that two or more organizational sponsors (for example, training, logistics, and manpower) have each proposed several items (for example, procurement packages, research programs, and the like) for funding. The items all compete with one another for consideration, and each item has benefits, both assessed by the item's sponsor group. The model also assumes that a group of independent judges ("honest brokers") has assigned a relative importance weight to one randomly selected item from each sponsor.

Each resource allocation model created by the user always consists of the following elements:

- ◆ Problem Area
- ◆ Organizational Sponsors
- ◆ Items
- ◆ Cost Components
- ◆ Item Costs
- ◆ Item Benefit
- ◆ Benefit Rationale
- ◆ Item Weights

The input specifications of the model can be processed to produce the following results:

> *Total cost*—a single number representing the total cost for each item.
>
> *Normalized benefit*—a single number representing the normalized benefit associated with items from the sponsors. The normalized benefit indicates the item's position relative to all items submitted by all of the sponsors. Normalized benefits range on a scale extending from 0 to 100.
>
> *Cost-benefit ratios*—a single number representing the ratio of cost to benefit for each item. This number is calculated by dividing the item's total cost by its normalized benefit.
>
> *Item rankings*—a single list representing the order in which the items should be acquired. The list is arranged according to the cost-benefit criterion (whereby items with the lowest ratio of cost to benefit are bought first). However, items designated as "must-buy" items (designated as such either for "political" considerations or because of contractual obligations) are always ranked first.
>
> *Cost-benefit versus benefit-only display*—a set of displays that shows the order in which the items would be bought both according to a cost-benefit criterion (buying in order of smallest to largest cost-benefit ratio) and according to a benefit-only criterion (buying in order of greatest to smallest overall benefit).
>
> *Cumulative cost display*—this display yields the cumulative cost, by cost component, as each item is acquired under a variety of criteria.

To illustrate how RAM can be used, consider the following Decisions and Designs, Inc. example. Assume first that a small company has two departments: production and marketing. In preparation for a budget review, each department has nominated several projects for funding. The departments have ranked the projects in order of their perceived benefit, as shown below:

PRODUCTION			MARKETING		
Rank	Project	Cost	Rank	Project	Cost
1	A	$60K	1	X	$80K
2	B	$40K	2	Y	$30K
3	C	$10K	3	Z	$20K
4	D	$12K			

Assume that the company has limited resources (sound familiar?) and can expend only $140K. Note that the total cost of all seven projects is $252K. The company must thus decide which of the seven projects to fund.

The initial step requires the departments to scale the benefits of their projects. A relative benefit value of 100 is assigned to the most beneficial project. The other projects are scaled accordingly (and supported by written rationale). Assume next that the projects are assigned the benefit values shown below (note that the costs are at this point excluded):

PRODUCTION		MARKETING	
Project	Benefit	Project	Benefit
A	100	X	100
B	50	Y	80
C	20	Z	25
D	15		

Note also that several implications arise from these scaled values. For example, the production department feels that funding project A will prove more beneficial than funding all of the remaining projects: B, C, and D. The marketing department feels that project Y is more than three times more beneficial than project Z. Several experts, referred to as "honest brokers," are briefed on the companywide benefits of one marketing project and one production project, the choice being random, but department-assigned benefit values are not communicated to the experts. Assume, for example, that the honest brokers have been briefed on projects C and Y. The honest brokers are then asked to rank-order and interval-scale the two projects. The results are shown below, where project C is judged to be 40% as beneficial as project Y:

Project	Company Benefit
Y	100
C	40

At this point, the relative benefits of the seven candidate projects have been established, as shown below:

Project	Benefit
A	100
X	62.5
B	50
Y	50
C	20
Z	15.6
D	15

The costs of the projects are then used to determine the prioritized list ordered by the cost-benefit ratio, as shown below:

Funding order	Project	Cost	Company benefit	Cost-benefit ratio
1	C	$10K	20	0.5
2	A	$60K	100	0.6
3	Y	$30K	50	0.6
4	B	$40K	50	0.8
5	D	$12K	15	0.8
6	X	$80K	62.5	1.3
7	Z	$20K	15.6	1.3

A line has been drawn at the pre-established funding constraint of $140K. But if the company had adopted their benefit-only policy, the final order would have been very different, as presented below:

Funding order	Project	cost	Company benefit
1	A	$60K	100
2	X	$80K	62.5
3	Y	$30K	50
4	B	$40K	50
5	C	$10K	20
6	Z	$20K	15.6
7	D	$12K	15

Again note the line drawn at the funding constraint of $140K. Note that for $140K the benefit-only prioritization provides a total company benefit of 162.5, whereas the cost-benefit prioritization provides a total benefit of 220, more than 35% more.

Linear and Dynamic Programming Allocation Methods

Linear programming methods can be applied to complicated resource allocation problems when, according to Robert J. Thierauf (*An Introductory Approach to Operations Research*, New York: John Wiley, 1978), the following conditions are met:

> *Linear Problem*—where the problem parameters constitute a linear function, for example, as with the relationships between item production costs and profits.
>
> *Alternative Allocation Strategies*—where alternative resource mixes are possible and at least intuitively viable.
>
> *Mathematical Expression*—of linear functions and linear constraints.
>
> *Interrelated Variables*—where mathematical relationships among the variables are easily described.
>
> *Limited Resources*—which are finite and quantifiable.

Very succinctly, linear programming enables a problem-solver to optimize the allocation of resources according to a specific goal. For example, imagine a small stationery factory which must determine an optimal production schedule for the upcoming month. Its two major products are pencils and pens. But the problem involves discovering the combination of the two goods which will yield the most profit. Profit on each pencil is 1¢, while each pen generates 5¢ profit. Monthly production times for pencils and pens across three workstations are as follows:

Workstation	Workstation capacity (hours)	Production time (minutes)	
		Pencils	Pens
1	2000	20	5
2	1600	14	3
3	1800	5	7

Given that profit can be expressed according to a simple formula (Profit = 1¢ pencil + 5¢ pen) and that the objective is to maximize profit, the linear programming method will calculate mathematically the optimal production schedule given the above production constraints across the three factory workstations. Specifically, the method will calculate exactly how many pencils and pens should be produced given the goal to maximize profit.

There are two primary linear programming methods: the graphic method and the extremely popular and powerful simplex method. The graphic method involves the plotting of the linear function and constraints in a multidimensional space and then solving the simultaneous equations of the plotted lines. The simplex method involves the implementation of an iterative mathematical process until the best solution (or optimal mix) is found. It is a complicated procedure too detailed to go into here, but, fortunately, there are a number of computer programs which can render painless a process which is complex even to sophisticated operations researchers.

Dynamic programming methods account for problem time intervals in a manner which linear programming cannot. Also, the mathematical procedures which underlie linear and dynamic programming are quite different.

Both procedures are extremely usefully applied to resource allocation problems when data, expertise, and computer support are *all* available. But when all of these elements are present, linear and dynamic programming can be extremely powerful tools.

COMPARATIVE EVALUATION METHODOLOGY

Predictive and prescriptive methodology can often be evaluated one against the other— with sometimes arbitrary results. In other words, some forecasting and prescriptive problems can actually be handled adequately by several methodologies. Evaluation problems infrequently present such flexibility. Subjective, or qualitative, evaluation methodology is generally applied to problems which are to some extent inherently qualitative. Objective methodology should be applied to problems which are inherently quantitative. Guidelines for the application of linear and dynamic programming methodology are even more explicit.

Nearly all of the evaluation methodology discussed here requires considerable support and expertise. Computer support is also almost always necessary, and, since evaluation is by definition organizationally and/or bureaucratically complex, one should be certain that all of the tools of problem-solving are available.

SUMMARY

Before an evaluation is launched, a thorough evaluability assessment should be made. This should involve assessments regarding how inherently amenable the object of evaluation is, whether the evaluation is to be of a process or an entity, and what the purpose of the evaluation is. Some assessment of the motives of those who commission the evaluation should also be made. Overt motives can take various forms, but covert ones usually serve other than analytical purposes. Subjective and objective evaluation methods are epistemologically similar to subjective and objective predictive and prescriptive methodology, but less flexibly applied than other methodologies. Interviews, working groups, and questionnaires can be used to generate evaluation data; multi-attribute utility modeling can be used to organize qualitative data in a way which recognizes weighted evaluative criteria and facilitates subjective entity evaluation against the criteria. Standard statistical techniques can be used to conduct quantitative-empirical process or entity evaluations, and cost-benefit, linear, and dynamic programming methodologies can be used for resource allocation evaluation problems. Fortunately, multi-attribute utility analysis, cost-benefit analysis, linear and dynamic programming, and nearly all of the standard descriptive and inferential statistical routines have been computerized successfully. EVAL and RAM represent two good examples of successful computerization. Finally, nearly all useful evaluations require a good deal of time, talent, expertise, support, and organizational effort.

BIBLIOGRAPHIC ESSAY

Evaluation is a multi-faceted enterprise. There is process evaluation and entity evaluation. Leonard Rutman's edited *Evaluation Research Methods* (Beverly Hills, CA: Sage Publications, 1977) is excellent for the former. In that volume, Rutman's "Planning an Evaluation Study," from which portions of this section were drawn, is particularly useful for process organization. Joseph S. Wholey's "Evaluability Assessment," also in the Rutman volume and also used to prepare this handbook, is especially good for assessing whether or not a process can be evaluated. Ernest R. House's

Evaluating with Validity (Beverly Hills, CA: Sage Publications, 1980) is also excellent, as are Michael Quinn Patton's *Qualitative Evaluation Methods* (Beverly Hills, CA: Sage Publications, 1980); Rutman's *Planning Useful Evaluations: Evaluability Assessment* (Beverly Hills, CA: Sage Publications, 1980); Mark Thompson's *Benefit-Cost Analysis for Program Evaluation* (Beverly Hills, CA: Sage Publications, 1980); Linda A. Allardyce, Dorothy M. Amey, Phillip H. Feuerwerger, and Roy M. Gulick's *Documentation of Decision-Aiding Software: EVAL Users Manual* (McLean, VA: Decisions and Designs, November 1979); Linda B. Allardyce, Dorothy M. Amey, Phillip H. Feuerwerger, and Roy M. Gulick's *Documentation of Decision-Aiding Software: EVAL Functional Description* (McLean, VA: Decisions and Designs, November 1979); Dorothy M. Amey, Phillip H. Feuerwerger, and Roy M. Gulick's *Documentation of Decision-Aiding Software: RAM Users Manual* (McLean, VA: Decisions and Designs, September 1979); Dorothy M. Amey, Phillip H. Feuerwerger, and Roy M. Gulick's *Documentation of Decision-Aiding Software: RAM Functional Description* (McLean, VA: Decisions and Designs, September 1979); and Ward Edwards' *How to Use Multi-Attribute Utility Measurement for Social Decision Making* (Los Angeles: Social Science Research Institute, University of Southern California, August 1976). Andrieu's "Benefit Cost Evaluation," in *Evaluation Research Methods* is also superb. R.J. Thierauf's *An Introductory Approach to Operations Research* (New York: John Wiley, 1978), and Richard E. Trueman's *An Introduction to Quantitative Methods for Decision Making* (New York: Holt, Rinehart and Winston, 1977) are both excellent sources for linear and dynamic programming. D.R. Anderson, D. Sweeney, and T.A. Williams' *Linear Programming for Decision Making: An Application Approach* (St. Paul, MN: West Publishing, 1976), and H.G. Dallenbach and E.J. Bell's *User's Guide to Linear Programming* (Englewood Cliffs, N.J.: Prentice-Hall, 1969) are also useful.

9

Documentation

PROBLEM SOLUTIONS which are poorly documented generally go unappreciated and unapplied. Indeed, it is difficult to underestimate the importance of documentation in the problem-solving process.

The most important form of documentation is the written record, including reports and memoranda.

REPORTS AND MEMORANDA

Most good problem-solvers are only mediocre report writers (and vice versa). Usually this is because problem-solvers are too close to the technical details of a problem; consequently, they often report upon matters, steps, and processes of little real interest to the original problem-generator and solution-consumer.

When a problem is identified and confirmed by a potential consumer, the problem-solver(s) usually go to work, ideally performing all of the organizational steps outlined in chapter 3. Hours, days, weeks, and even months later, he or she is perhaps light years away from the single, straightforward solution the problem-generator perceives as forthcoming. The written record of the problem-solving process must thus disconnect its genesis from its evolution and explicitly focus upon the end product.

If requirements analyses are performed often and competently, and yield useful insights into what it is a particular problem-generator does, then many of the disconnect problems can be avoided.

There are a number of techniques and procedures which can be implemented to ensure that one's report actually reports upon items of direct interest and use to solution-consumers. First, unless a problem-solver is an especially talented technical summarizer, synthesizer, writer, and editor, it usually pays to commission an "outsider" to at least participate in the preparation of the report. However, this does not necessarily mean that an outside consultant be hired; rather, only that it is helpful to acquire the services of someone who has not walked each and every step of the problem-solving path alongside of the principal investigator. A research assistant or colleague from a related department or office could provide invaluable assistance reading drafts and making recommendations about clarity and brevity.

The first step toward the compilation of a formal report is organization, and the most important component of organization is the outline. Following the assembly of all pertinent facts and results, the report writer should develop a topical, sentence, or paragraph outline. Each kind has its strengths and weaknesses; report writers should experiment with them all until a preference is discovered. The outline method itself should be consistent with whatever report format is preferred by your office, department, agency, or organization. For example, if established report format requires numeric headings and subheadings (1.0, 1.1, 1.1.1, and so forth), then the outline should be so developed.

In addition, reports should *always* be preceeded by an *overview* or *executive summary* comprised of a *brief problem statement*, a *brief summary of the findings and recommendations*, a *brief nontechnical discussion of the approaches and methods used to solve the problem*, and lastly but straightforwardly, a *summary and brief description of the caveats which apply*. The overview/executive summary should be followed by the report itself which addresses *all* of the components of the overview/executive summary in considerably more detail. However, unless the report is prepared explicitly for very technical consumers, highly technical information should appear only in appendices.

Another absolutely critical aspect of report preparation concerns the level of discourse. Frequently, problem-solvers, in an effort to impress others, will make use of technical jargon, awkward academic phrasing, pointless pedantics, unjustified neologizing, and confusing mixed (and unmixed) metaphors. Like the above sentence, such discourse serves no purpose, save perhaps making a simple point the hard way. Note, for example, the differences between some old and new legal phrasing by an all too familiar tax gathering federal agency.

OLD

An increase or decrease in the income of an eligible individual or his eligible spouse, the ineligible spouse living with the eligible individual, the parent or spouse or such parent living with an eligible individual who is a child, an ineligible child living in the same household as an eligible individual or an essential person must be reported.

NEW

You must report to us any increase or decrease in your income, and any increase or decrease in the income of:

♦ Your ineligible spouse who lives with you;

♦ Your essential person;

♦ Your parent, if you are an eligible child and your parent lives with you; or

♦ An ineligible child who lives with you.

The lesson above is clear. Not only should we search for the most easily understood phraseology, but we should also be aware of the impact which format can exert upon understanding. Above all else, then, we should remember that the function of words is to communicate. If they are improperly or carelessly used, they will betray their users.

A final point concerns appearance. All reports and memoranda should look as good as they read. As everyone knows, a physically unattractive document will go unread. Great care should be taken to package solutions carefully and attractively. Typographical errors, poorly prepared illustrations, and haphazardly assembled reports and memoranda only contribute to already declining professional problem-solving standards.

Above all else, every problem-solving document must address the predetermined problem requirement(s) as explicitly as possible in clear, concise language which fills the clean pages of a neatly prepared report.

Sometimes a summary memorandum can substitute nicely for a more formal report. Memoranda are preferable in principle because they are much less imposing than larger, heavier reports. In other words, a short, attractive memorandum is frequently more likely to be read than a long report. More specifically, there are several memorandum writing techniques which can enhance comprehension and assimilation by a problem-consumer. The first is the

♦ summary "bullet."

Bullets can raise to the forefront a fact or statement which might otherwise remain buried in the body of the text. One should avoid, however, "bulletizing" too much. Type font variation is another highlighting technique made possible by computer-based word processing systems and interchangeable typing elements, as is <u>underlining</u> and standard indentation and set-off techniques. Finally, the prudent use of graphic illustrations can often make a point more poignantly than words. Tables are effective communications tools at times as well.

The following steps are thus necessary to compile a useful report or memorandum:

♦ Organize
♦ Outline
♦ Format
   Executive summary
   Main body
   Concise conclusion(s)
♦ Maintain Appropriate Level of Discourse
♦ Judicious Use of Figures, Tables, "Bullets," Type Fonts, and Other Highlighting Techniques

VERBAL PRESENTATIONS

More often than not consumers want to be told about solutions. Frequently too busy (or, candidly, lazy) to read even short memoranda, and eager to "hold court," they schedule long meetings to hear (and challenge in front of an audience) all about the problem-solver's findings. Consequently, problem-solvers must be prepared to present their findings effectively and persuasively (more on this point in chapter 10). The key aspects of verbal presentations are succinctness, clarity, and economy of discourse. Generally, the verbal presentation should reflect the written record in order to prevent later contradictions and confusion. The presentation should consist of a brief overview/executive summary and then concise statements about the project's technical approach and methodology. One should be extremely careful, however, not to inject personal biases and emotional fact-free arguments. *Stick to the script*! Also, pay special attention to linking the findings to the original requirements. Refuse to be dissuaded from describing the project's primary problem-solving purposes. *Avoid tangents*. Avoid answering unasked questions as well as those poorly presented, and beware of traps. Since in some cases a long period of time may have passed between the time the work began and the verbal presentation of the findings, and since attitudes may have changed, the consumers may have substantially different motives in mind than when they originally conceived of the project.

Verbal presentations should thus adhere to the following guidelines:

- Succinctness
- Clarity
- Economy of Discourse
- Objectivity
- Consistency

DISTRIBUTION

It is important to know to whom to distribute findings and who to avoid. By and large, the generators, consumers, and their staffs should all receive written and verbal reports. But where should one stop? For example, should the superiors of the consumers receive copies? Generally, they should not (unless, of course, one has specific instructions to do so) because the superior may or may not be aware of the project (and may in fact even be unaware of the problem). Distribution to superiors can disrupt relations with the problem-generators and, indirectly, with the problem-solvers.

On the other hand, sometimes selected distribution of reports can greatly enhance a problem-solver's image and reputation. At the very least, selected distribution can advertise that a particular problem-solver is alive and well in environments where he or she might not be very familiar or well known. Distribution can also serve to cross-fertilize and cross-pollinate ideas across many fields of analysis and contribute to future problem-solving effectiveness.

The *distribution list* is a good tool for maximizing controlled exposure. Like data and talent inventories, such lists should be maintained and updated according to substantive (and bureaucratic) categories and imperatives.

Yet another form of distribution is much more public. Here the reference is to the publication of findings in recognized journals, magazines, and newsletters. Some major projects can often be converted to monograph or book form. Indeed, it is sad to see so many well-conceived and well-executed projects go uncommunicated to the outside world, especially since publication can pay large professional dividends to the authors and the organizations to which they belong. Future credibility can be dramatically enhanced by just one by-line.

Guidelines for the effective distribution of reports and memoranda include *control* and *selectivity*.

UNCONVENTIONAL DOCUMENTATION

It is appropriate here to discuss some unconventional documentation techniques. Recently, the use of videotape, videodiscs, 35MM slides, overhead viewgraphs, and tape recordings to document projects is increasing. Instead of long written documents, problem-solvers are now filming themselves presenting their findings. They are also submitting taped cassettes of their work to consumers in order to give consumers the convenience of hearing about the work while dressing, driving, or relaxing. Finally, more and more frequently problem-solvers are submitting packs of 35MM slides and/or stacks of viewgraphs to consumers in attempts to present visually what they prefer not to present textually.

While there are many problems connected with such unconventional documentation, there are many advantages as well. For example, nonroutine documentation, used strategically, can catapult a particular project into a new and desirable spotlight. It can also lead to new modes of expression, and can frequently be prepared in much less time than it takes to prepare conventional written reports (provided that the necessary human and mechanical equipment is available).

In any case, problem-solvers should be aware of the following unconventional documentation techniques and how they can be used to accentuate analytical findings:

- ♦ Videotape
- ♦ Videodiscs
- ♦ 35MM Slides
- ♦ Overhead Viewgraphs
- ♦ Tape Recordings

SUMMARY

Perhaps the most important aspect of written and verbal documentation is targeting. At all times, an effort must be made to link the solution to its problem in a manner which results in unencumbered communication. The use of language is as important as the use of graphic figures and tables. During verbal presentations it is necessary to remain logical, consistent, and objective; and when all else fails, perhaps it is time to experiment with some unconventional documentation techniques. Distribution is also an important element of the documentation process. But distribution should always be selective. Finally, if documentation looks or sounds bad, it should go unreported.

BIBLIOGRAPHIC ESSAY

There is no shortage of books, articles, monographs, or training seminars on effective writing. Nor is there a shortage of complaints about bad writing. For example, the editor-in-chief of *Byte*, an information systems magazine, recently asked in an ever-timely editorial, "What's Wrong with Technical Writing Today?" (*Byte*, December 1980, pp. 5–10). Among other failings, Chris Morgan complained about the excessive use of the passive voice, big words when small ones will do, and unclear instructions to the reader. On the positive side, Morgan suggests that verbs be used without adverbs, that all text be broken up into "digestible chunks," that theme sentences be used to introduce long sections or chapters, and that writers attempt to place themselves in the minds of the readers while they are writing. In another trade piece, Ann-Marie Lamb's "Seven Ways to Better Client Reports, Presentations" (*Infosystems*, May 1980, pp. 84–9) stresses the elimination of jargon, the institutionalization of in-house reviews of reports and major memoranda, and systemic report and presentation planning. On a more formal level is Courtland L. Bovee's *Business Writing Workshop* (La Mesa, Ca: Roxbury Publishing, 1980); David W. Ewing's *Writing for Results* (New York: Wiley-Interscience, 1970); John P. Riebel's *How to Write Reports, Theses, Articles* (New York: Arco Publishing, 1978); Carolyn J. Mullins' *The Complete Writing Guide to Preparing Reports, Proposals, Memos, Etc.* (Englewood Cliffs, N.J.: Prentice-Hall, 1980); H.J. Tichy's *Effective Writing for Managers, Engineers, Scientists* (New York: John Wiley, 1966); Burton L. Fischman's *Business Report Writing* (Providence, R.I.: P.A.R., 1975); and Lassar A. Blumenthal's *Successful Business Writing* (New York: Grosset and Dunlap, 1976). All are very good. Some less focused classics include, William Strunk, Jr. and E.B. White's *The Elements of Style* (New York: Macmillan, 1962); Sheriden Baker's *The Complete Stylist* (New York: Thomas Y. Crowell, 1966); and Glenn Leggett, David Mead, and William Charvat's *Handbook for Writers* (Englewood Cliffs, N.J.: Prentice-Hall, 1978). The effective use of graphic and tabular information in reports and presentations will become apparent following a perusal of Calvin F. Schmid's *Handbook of Graphic Presentation* (New York: John Wiley, 1979), and A. Lockwood's *Diagrams: A Visual Survey of Graphs, Maps, Charts, and Diagrams for the Graphic Designer* (Vista, N.Y.: Watson-Guptill, 1977). Similarly, Jane Wollman's "Video as a Sales Tool" (*Output*, April 1981, pp. 28–32) gives a feel for how to use videocassette tapes, videodiscs, closed circuit television, two-way television, and teletext effectively.

10

Defense

DOCUMENTATION COMPRISES but half of the communications process. Frequently, problem-solvers must defend their research in varied environments where multiple and sometimes hostile motives may be at work. Consequently, problem-solvers must be completely cognizant of the importance and mechanics of briefings, argumentation, negotiation, and the bureaucratic milieu in which all of these activities must take place.

BRIEFINGS

As discussed briefly in chapter 9, verbal presentations are often of critical importance to the problem-solver process. As the list below suggests, however, successful briefings are comprised of many distinct components:

- ◆ Audience Profiling
- ◆ Problem Statement
- ◆ Clarity
- ◆ Brevity
- ◆ Responsiveness

Above all else, problem-solvers must be intimately familiar with the audience to which the briefing is to be given. This familiarity enables a problem-solver to structure and present his or her briefing in the most receptive manner possible. For example, briefings given to high-level nontechnical managerial types should be virtually devoid of technical content. Conversely, technicrats frequently are less interested in the overall motivations and/or goals of the project being briefed and are content to dwell upon minute technical details. Secondly, the problem should be extremely well and concisely stated. Not unlike the assembly of a good report or memorandum, all briefings should begin with general statements about the origins, nature, purpose, and findings of the project being briefed. Depending upon the audience, the project can be analyzed and explored briefly and/or in-depth. Of paramount importance is the logic or reasoning which must underlie all verbal presentations. In short, if a briefing doesn't "flow" it will be of little value to the problem-solver or the solution-consumers. Obtusive and/or jargonized language is almost always self-defeating.

Like all structured presentations, briefings must be developed and tested. More specifically, briefings must be comprised of a coherent introduction, a modular middle, and a forthright ending. The introduction should first be comprised of a list of contents so that the briefees know how far and how long the briefing can be expected to go. The problem should be stated briefly and lucidly. Moreover, the briefing's conclusion should be presented during the introduction. The high or low technical content should be prepared in a modular way, that is, in a way which enables a briefer to go into more or less technical detail if the occasion arises. Frequently, for example, a briefer will be interrupted in the middle of a presentation by someone questioning an aspect of the briefing which is not explicitly evident in the presentation. Here, back-up material should be available for insertion. The briefing's conclusion should be comprised of whatever caveats apply to the "findings." If appropriate, the conclusion should also contain a list of projects which should be undertaken as an extension of the initial project.

Since all verbal presentations are people-intensive, it is important that the briefer be perceived as a real and interested person. Among other positive characteristics, briefers should always be at least perceived as sincere. A lackluster, disinterested, and otherwise boring performance on the part of the briefer can undermine even the most successfully conducted project. Briefings should thus only be presented by articulate, aggressive, energetic, and knowledgeable persons.

Finally, questions which arise during and after a briefing must be answered directly. Unlike candidates running for political office, briefers should never revel in the vague or understated. If a specific question cannot be answered, then it should be so acknowledged. If more time is needed to answer a specific question, then request it. Also, it is always a good idea to ask the questioner if he or she is satisfied with the answer. If so, then you can move on to additional questions; and if not, you can try again. One should never, however, avoid answering a question or present to a questioner an unsatisfactory answer.

Like all presentations, briefings involve strategy and tactics. If this sounds too contrived, remember that during a briefing everyone is playing roles that are more or less expected of them. Sometimes these roles can be deliberately hostile. One should thus approach a briefing as though it were an encounter of wills. Briefers should "dry-run" all presentations. They should also be especially aware of how long a briefing will take, recognizing along the way that a briefing which lasts longer than one hour is likely to be ineffective. If a briefer works in a particularly harried environment where briefees are continually interrupted and never seem to have enough time to hear the whole story, then the overscheduling technique should be used. Briefly, overscheduling simply involves making a prior appointment with the key briefees immediately following the conclusion of the briefing. Consequently, if the briefing runs longer than anticipated, the briefees have no excuse to leave and reschedule.

The clever use of audiovisual aids is also of paramount importance. Colorful view-graphs, 35mm slides, and the like can, when skillfully used, create a comfortable and entertaining atmosphere. For those who subscribe to the research regarding the specific use of color, keep in mind that bright orange is considered by most psychologists to evoke tension and the softer pastels calm and relaxation. However, if one relies heavily upon the use of audiovisual aids, then back-up systems ought to be available in case of failure.

Another technique which is grounded in psychological research suggests that briefings should never be given by a single individual; rather, the briefers should tag-team the presentation. More specifically, psychological research indicates that each time a new speaker appears during a briefing, interest in the material is heightened. As a general rule, it is useful to mix-and-match the briefers to include old, young, male, and female presenters.

If a briefing must last for more than one hour, it is a good idea to provide refreshments and other "distractions." Not only will the availability of refreshments discourage "unauthorized" interruptions, but it will also contribute to a positive briefing atmosphere.

While one should stick fairly closely to the suggestions presented above regarding the development and structuring of a briefing, when there are many and varied topics to be covered it is important to understand the strategy and tactics connected with the ordering of the material. Clearly, if the primary purpose of the briefing is to brief two or three major topics, they should not be last on the agenda. Similarly, the most articulate and experienced briefers should always brief the most important topics.

Provisions should also always be made for the monitoring of the briefing by members of the briefing team. Here the reference is to the recording of questions asked and the scoring of how well the briefers deal with the questions. Specific technical comments made by the briefees should also be noted as well as any requests for additional information that they may make during the briefing. In effect, the monitoring technique requires members of the briefing team to watch themselves and the briefees and to note how the performance might be improved in the future. Some organizations and groups have even gone so far as to videotape their own presentations for later analysis.

Finally, it is important to arrange a debriefing after the presentation has concluded. The debriefing should not take place immediately following the briefing but several days later. The primary purpose of the debriefing is to receive feedback from the key briefees regarding how well or how badly the presentation was received. Debriefings can be of enormous help in planning future presentations. They also enable briefees to say privately what they might have been reluctant to say during the formal presentation.

The list below summarizes all of these briefing "tools and tricks":

♦ Dry-running
♦ Timing and Overscheduling

- ◆ Audiovisuals
- ◆ Tag-teaming
- ◆ Refreshments and Other Distractions
- ◆ Agendizing
- ◆ Monitoring
- ◆ Debriefing and Feedback

ARGUMENTATION AND NEGOTIATION

Argumentation is comprised of debating and successful debating is in turn comprised of persuasiveness. In formal terms, argumentation consists of reasons given by people in communicative situations. Debating is the process of inquiry and advocacy, seeking reasoned judgment on a proposition; and, according to Aristotle, persuasion is comprised first of the character of the speaker, second, the attitude in the hearer, and, third, the argument proper.

Aristotle's observation is insightful. Not only is the argument itself important during the process of argumentation but the attitudes of the speaker and the hearer are just as important. Accordingly, one must endeavor to create the right context and perspective upon which to build an effective argument. In other words, logic is only one of the tools for successful argumentation.

Nevertheless, one should pay special attention to the processes of logical argument formation and presentation. Non sequiturs, for example, serve no purpose. Not only should effective argumentation be evident during verbal presentations, but it should be high-profiled in written reports and memoranda as well. Indeed, the logic and reasoning which underlie effective argumentation should be present throughout the entire problem-solving process.

It is especially important to understand the nature and role of opposing perceptions during the argumentation process. As discussed above in the prescription section, images, perceptions, values, and the like all influence human cognitive activity. Perhaps nowhere is the influence so great as during an argument.

At the very least, one should emerge from an argument victorious, even at the expense of one's opponent. However, this is by no means a desirable outcome. Instead, the goal should always be to persuade one's opponent regarding the merits of one's argument. Indeed, much argumentation will evolve in conducive settings into negotiations. Still, one should at all times be aware of the process of refutation which almost always involves undermining the "opposition's" argument via the skillful use of logic, new evidence, and superior reasoning.

If a negotiation is to ensue, then we should all be aware that negotiations are not games or wars. In a successful negotiation, everybody wins something. At all cost must the "bad outcome," where one emerges feeling superior and the other plotting revenge, be avoided.

In a very real sense skilled negotiators are also skilled debaters, while skilled debaters are less frequently successful negotiators. Negotiations often require as many varied and polished personal skills as they do skills of logic and reason.

Perhaps the most challenging aspect of successful argumentation and negotiation lies with the inhibition of one's own ego and narrow goals. Some of the requisite attitudes to successful argumentation and negotiation include the desire to solve a problem even if it is embarrassing or awkward, the desire and ability to listen to one's colleagues, and a pre-disposition to accuracy and fact. Obviously, few of us are always in command of such attitudes. Nevertheless, since the problem-solving process is increasingly becoming organizational- and people-intensive, we have little choice but to acquiesce to our environment. In the long run, when style and form fade, the substance and content of successful arguments will endure. At the same time, "bureaucratic politics" often provides a frustrating backdrop for honest negotiations. In response, the best we can do is to acknowledge and attempt to understand bureaucratic and organizational phenomena to the point where we can (a) expose them and (b) manipulate them away from problem-solving influence.

The processes of argumentation and negotiation are of enormous importance to the defense of research results and to the larger problem-solving process. Cynics are quick to point out, however, that personality should never dominate the problem-solving process and that we should spend more time perfecting our methodological skills and a lot less worrying about how to "best" old Charlie down the hall. The position here is one of balance. While we should continually strive to improve our methodological skills, we must at the same time develop the skills so necessary for analytical closure, including especially at least a rudimentary understanding of basic argumentation and negotiation.

"BUREAUCRATIC POLITICS"

The federal government is not the only place where one can find out-of-control bureaucratic behavior. Nearly all organizations of five or more people are plagued by procedure and Murphy's Law. Formally, bureaucracies are characterized by sets of fixed rules which govern the behavior of official participants who engage in more or less regular activities. Authority is always arranged hierarchically. In principle, bureaucratic rules are supposed to ease procedural problems, but unfortunately somewhere along the line bureaucratic and other organizations evolved into living, functioning entities capable of thwarting even the best intentions. One of the classic expressions of bureaucratic influence has to do with the roles that each of us plays within a bureaucracy or an organization. Sociologists have long argued that bureaucracies have so developed that one's individual identity is completely dependent upon one's bureaucratic or organizational role. The sad implication of this conclusion is that individuals within organizations and bureaucracies infrequently respond to individuals but rather almost always deal with the roles created within the bureaucratic or organizational structure. Consequently, it is often extremely difficult to operate as an individual within a large organization or bureaucracy. One is almost always constrained by the policies, procedures, rules, and regulations which in essence comprise the organization.

Problem-solvers who are not managers suffer the greatest within bureaucratic organizations. Since their goals and modi operandi are by definition alien to bureaucratic structures, they are frequently frustrated by rules and regulations perceived to be irrelevant at best and downright inhibiting at worst. Managers who are not simultaneously problem-solvers also suffer from bureaucratic constraints, since they are frequently only able to see how a problem or problem solution "fits" within existing bureaucratic structures. The position here is that bureaucracies in their dominant form are by and large inhibiting to the problem-solving process. Problem-solvers must thus remain acutely aware of the environment in which they operate and when necessary able to maneuver themselves successfully through the environment.

Bureaucracies also contribute to incentive problems. All too often veteran bureaucrats discover that the only real bureaucratic rewards are gained exclusively through manipulation of the "rules." They thus orient their behavior and goals around the rules. Unfortunately, instead of contributing to efforts to subjugate the bureaucracy, such behavior actually contributes to its autonomous life. Problem-solvers should thus view bureaucratic constraints as necessary and real obstacles to successful problem-solving, not as the tools by which they might gain additional personal power and prestige.

SUMMARY

Defense of one kind or another is almost always necessary. Problem-solvers must thus develop their briefing skills to the point where they can comfortably and effectively communicate verbally to those whom they must inspire, impress, or influence. While verbal skills are essential to successful briefings, they must be accompanied by solid planning and logistical skills. Argumentation and negotiation skills are also necessary. But perhaps equally important is the bureaucratic milieu in which all such skills must be used. Managers and project administrators should be continually on the look-out for articulate briefers, debaters, and negotiators. They can contribute as much to the problem-solving process as the best methodologist.

BIBLIOGRAPHIC ESSAY

Briefings, argumentation, negotiations, and "bureaucratic politics" are complicated and diverse subjects. Yet a number of good sources exist. For a theoretical look at verbal communication, by all means see Kathleen Kelley Reardon's *Persuasion: Theory and Context* (Beverly Hills, Ca: Sage Publications, 1981); Michael E. Roloff and Gerald R. Miller's edited *Persuasion: New Directions in Theory and Research* (Beverly Hills, Ca: Sage Publications, 1980); Susan B. Shimanoff's *Communications Rules: Theory and Research* (Beverly Hills, Ca: Sage Publications; 1980), Dean C. Barnlund's *Interpersonal Communication: Survey and Studies* (Boston: Houghton Mifflin, 1969); and Austin J. Freeley's *Argumentation and Debate: Rational Decision Making* (Belmont, Ca: Wadsworth Publishing, 1976). Much less scholarly are Herb Cohen's *You Can Negotiate Anything* (Secaucus, N.J.: Lyle Stuart, 1980), and Michael D. McMaster and John Grinder's "The Art of Communicating" (*Computer Decisions*, December 1980, pp. 54-8). Gerald L. Nierenberg's *The Art of Negotiating* (New York: Cornerstone Library, 1968), William S. Tacey's *Business and Professional Speaking* (Dubuque, Iowa: William C. Brown, 1980), and Paul Watzlawick, Janet Beavin, and Don Jackson's *The Pragmatics of Human Communication* (New York: W.W. Norton, 1967) are all also very useful. Some excellent sources on "bureaucratic politics" include Francis Rourke's *Bureaucracy, Politics, and Public Policy* (Boston: Little, Brown, 1969); Amitai Etzioni's *A Comparative Study of Complex Organizations* (Glencoe, N.Y.: The Free Press, 1961); Michael Crozier's *The Bureaucratic Phenomenon* (Chicago: University of Chicago Press, 1964); D. Katz and R. Kahn's *The Social Psychology of Organizations* (New York: John Wiley and Sons, 1966); and Dale Rhodabarger's "Are They Calling You A Bureaucrat" (*Computer Decisions*, March 1981, pp. 66-71). The U.S. Navy Publications and Printing Service recently published one of the very few briefing guides available today. Entitled, "Don't Talk. . . Communicate" (Washington, D.C.: Department of the Navy NAV PUB P3150-1-2-78), it deals explicitly with audience analysis, how to write a presentation, how and why to use visual aids, and how to rehearse, stage, and deliver a briefing.

11

Computers and Problem-Solving

THERE IS ABSOLUTELY no question that every single aspect of the problem-solving process as described above can be addressed productively through the use of computers. It is possible to compile and assess the tools of problem-solving with computers. It is possible to conduct requirements and constraint analyses easily with computers. In some instances, the conduct of descriptive, predictive, explanatory, prescriptive, and evaluative analyses can be made trivial through the use of computers. Statistical techniques which only ten years ago were beyond the reach of most problem-solvers can now be implemented interactively at a computer terminal. Charts, tables, diagrams, and administrative forms can all be easily generated through the use of computers. Finally, the distribution and defense of research results can be accomplished with computers.

In a very real and practical sense it is difficult to overestimate the potential use of computers for all kinds of problem-solving. Historically, however, this was not always the case. Just fifteen years ago computers were used primarily by large corporations and some government bureaucracies to solve but a few data intensive problems. In the early years computers were used primarily to store and analyze data in ways which today we would regard as elementary. Fifteen years ago computers were almost impossible to use by those untrained in computer science and operations. Moreover, computing costs were prohibitive for even medium-sized corporations and bureaucracies.

In the 1960s, computers were used by problem-solvers primarily in the batch mode. Batch computing required users to first write computer programs (in but a few languages), transfer their data onto computer cards, and then submit the "job" and wait for the results. Those who have used computers in this way can remember what seemed to be strange little people who lived behind small makeshift windows to which large stacks of computer cards were given. If you were lucky, you could pick up your results in a few hours; usually, however, you had to wait at least a day for the computer operators to "run your job."

Batch computing was for many an introduction to computing itself. By and large, it was slow and inefficient, and convinced too many of us that computers were not really all that useful. Consequently, too many problem-solvers developed a negative image about the advantages of computer-based and/or computer-assisted problem-solving.

Since the 1960s, however, staggering progress has been made. Through the introduction and perfection of macrocomputer systems, such as the early UNIVAC 1108 and the much more recent IBM 370, problem solvers are now able to conduct complicated analyses interactively at the computer terminal. In addition, through the introduction of minicomputers, such as the Digital Equipment Corporation's PDP 11/70, more and more businesses and agencies can afford their own in-house computers.

The real breakthrough came in the area of time-sharing, which enabled many users to simultaneously access the same computer programs and data bases. Another milestone may be found in the refinement of software languages and the resultant construction of innumerable applications programs. Such programs have enabled countless individuals to conduct sophisticated analyses in "real-time."

The revolution in computing has progressed so far that virtually every administrative, managerial, and analytical task imaginable has been computerized to the point where anyone with a few days training can interactively process enormous amounts of information in order to solve extremely specific problems.

While all of this may sound technologically impressive, most would argue today that the revolution in computer science and applied computing has only just begun. An extremely strong argument can be made, for example, that by 1990 computers will dominate most every aspect of our personal and professional lives. On the personal side, it will not be unusual for us to wake up in the morning, lean over to our night-tables, and control an unlimited number of household functions simply by depressing one key of an uncomplicated keyboard or, better yet, by simple voice commands. Not only will the computer execute our commands but in all likelihood it will speak to us along the way. On the professional side, it will not at all be unusual for individual problem-solvers to command their own personal computers which will be able to perform functions which twenty years ago could only be performed by room-size computers.

The revolution in computer science which will make all of this possible is the continued development of the integrated circuit or chip, which is the essence of today's and tomorrow's microcomputer. Chips have already made it possible to build computers which can easily fit into a briefcase. Indeed, hand-held computers are now on the market.

The implications of this revolution for analytical problem-solving are boundless. Virtually every methodology discussed in this handbook will be accessible via an easy to use and efficient computer program which in all likelihood will reside on a microcomputer. Today, for example, there are computer programs which enable problem-solvers to diagram and solve decision tree problems. There are also programs which enable forecasters to engage in simple Bayesian updating, Bayesian probability diagramming, and Bayesian hierarchical inference structuring. Similarly, there are microcomputer programs which enable users to perform correlational and regression analyses, as well as time-series, Box-Jenkins, and virtually all forms of extrapolative analyses. In addition, with the introduction of hard disk drive systems, problem-solvers can now store, retrieve, and analyze massive amounts of data, data previously only accessible via macro- and/or minicomputer systems.

INTERACTIVE VERSUS BATCH COMPUTING

As discussed briefly above, in the 1960s and early 1970s problem-solvers who relied upon computers generally did so in a batch mode whereby they would submit their data to a large computer system for analysis. Interactive time-sharing and individual computing has changed the very nature by which problem-solvers compute. Now it is possible to sit in front of a computer terminal and see the results of one's analyses in a matter of seconds. Obviously, then, the processes of computer-based problem-solving have been dramatically improved and accelerated. It is possible for a problem-solver to immediately see the results of, for example, a regression equation and then vary the weights in the equation in order to perform an immediate sensitivity analysis. "What-if" questions can be answered in seconds.

Interactive computing has had another effect as well. Many problem-solvers, previously predisposed against computer-based analysis, have begun to change their attitudes about computing. This shift has occurred primarily because the designers and developers of interactive computer systems have paid increasing attention to the needs, likes, and dislikes of the intended user. This movement toward improved "man-computer relations" has seen the introduction of voice input and output systems, natural language command systems, and interactive color graphic displays—all designed explicitly to improve the overall computing experience.

Interactive computing has also had an effect on the distribution of computer resources through time-sharing and, more recently, the development of the microprocessor. Now even small businesses maintain their own mini- and microcomputer systems.

The differences between batch and interactive processing can be summarized as follows:

Batch Processing	Interactive Processing
Slow	Time-shared and local
Restricted access	Fast
Expensive	"Personal"
	Distributed
	Relatively inexpensive

ADVANTAGES OF COMPUTER-BASED PROBLEM-SOLVING

Problem-solving can be enhanced by computers because computers can *routinize* many tasks and functions which are performed frequently. This can be done in two ways. First, by writing a new computer program to perform the repeated task and, second, by fitting an existing program to the task(s). Both ways can be costly, but if a set of tasks are truly repetitive then the costs may well prove negligible over the long run.

Another advantage of computer-based problem-solving is *documentation*, or "*audit-trailing*." Nearly all computer-based problem-solving produces a "hard" copy of the analysis as well as a capability to store the entire process. This capability enables problem-solvers to study analyses after the fact and pass on to successors an "institutional memory" of past analyses.

Computer-based analyses can often aid the *presentation* and *distribution* of findings as well. Presentation can be aided dramatically by computer-generated charts, graphs, diagrams, and even explanations, and distribution can be made easier by computer printers capable of generating and regenerating analyses and by electronic mailing systems which can automatically distribute data, research, and findings to everyone on a particular time-sharing system.

Computers can also reduce the requirements placed upon *support staff* by alleviating production pressures.

Problem-solvers can *learn* a great deal from computer-based problem-solving since *good* programs tend to guide and instruct their users. Consequently, the *range* of analytical methodologies which might be considered by problem-solvers can be increased via computer-based problem-solving.

Finally, imaginative *hybrid solutions* are often stimulated through computer-based problem-solving in ways unlike conventional brainstorming. Since it is so easy to analyze, reanalyze, combine, and compare through computing, novel applications are more easily discovered—and stored for future use.

The software which makes all of this possible is readily generated (through professional programmers) and available "off-the-shelf" (either free or for nominal, one-time, or licensing charges). For example, just about every primary statistical routine can be implemented via a software system known as SPSS (Statistical Package for the Social Sciences). Developed initially for social scientists, but extremely useful to anyone who uses statistics to solve problems, SPSS is an integrated set of computer programs for the analysis of quantitative data. Specifically, SPSS permits data transformation and file manipulation, and enables problem-solvers to conduct countless unsophisticated and sophisticated data analyses, including correlation (for both ordinal and interval data), partial correlation, means and variances, one-way and n-way analysis of variance, multiple regression, discriminate analysis, scatter diagrams, factor analysis, and canonical correlations. In addition to SPSS are a number of other statistical systems which can assist problem-solvers that will run on a variety of macro- and minicomputer systems, and with some additional programming can be made to run on many more.

Other "off-the-shelf" programs exist to help the problem-solver implement virtually all of the subjective forecasting methodologies discussed in chapter 6. Some of these programs are available free of charge while others must be purchased. For example, programs now exist for using Bayes' theorem, building and exercising probability diagrams and hierarchical inference structures, and conducting Delphi surveys. They are all free (see the Bibliographic Essay at the end of this chapter); and with an existing data set, problem-solvers can address a wide range of problems quickly and efficiently.

On the hardware side, the advantages of computer-based problem-solving can be seen in the physical size and power of the microcomputer. For example, the Radio Shack TRS-80 and Apple II computer systems both weigh less than fifty pounds and are easily mounted on a standard desk-top. Many other portable microcomputers are also available at surprisingly low cost. More important are the computer programs available for these systems. Many of them are inexpensive and relatively easy to use.

The advantages of computer-based problem-solving can be summarized as follows:

- ◆ Accelerated Routinized Problem-Solving
- ◆ Problem-Solving Documentation
- ◆ Presentations
- ◆ Distribution
- ◆ Support
- ◆ Off-the-shelf Applications Programs

DISADVANTAGES OF COMPUTER-BASED PROBLEM-SOLVING

Nothing is perfect. Where there are successes, there are failures. In the computer-based problem-solving area, failures include software incompatibility, hardware incompatibility, poor service, "good versus great" programmers, oversell, poor "man-machine relations," and pure misuse.

Software incompatibility across computer systems, languages and expertise is perhaps the single largest inhibiting force in the distribution of computer-based problem-solving. Each time a piece of software is transferred, modifications must be made if the version of the software and machine are different from those employed during the initial development. This problem is compounded because not only are there many different software languages but many different versions of each language as well. The same problems arise when one attempts to move a piece of software from one computer to another, since hardware too has its own particular capabilities and limitations. In short, whenever one tries to acquire and use a piece of ready-made software, one must confront sometimes large—and costly—software and hardware problems.

Service is also a problem. Frequently the author of a particular piece of applications or systems software, or the manufacturer of some hardware, are relatively disinterested in servicing what they sell, and often when they are interested they are unable to perform competent service (except for outrageously high costs).

Another problem is the quality of programmers available today. While there are many competent ones, anyone who has worked in the field knows how competent a good programmer is (or is not) in comparison to a great one. Perhaps in no other field is the difference so great. A good programmer can write a 1,000-line program in several months. In all likelihood it will run but it will not be without problems. A great programmer can write the same program in a month, use half of the lines, and produce a bug-free product. Good (and, obviously, bad) programmers can disappoint eager users, while great ones can stimulate even the disinterested problem-solver. Unfortunately, great programmers are rare; good ones proliferate the field; and bad ones are everywhere.

Still another problem is oversell. True believers can be overwhelming—and dangerous. Far too many proponents of computing believe that a problem has yet to be discovered which cannot be solved with a computer. Obviously wrong, they are often able to convince users that a panacea lies just beneath an alphanumeric keyboard. Consequently, many first time (and even veteran) computer users are misled into believing that computers can solve all of their problems. Computer vendors are also notorious oversellers. Almost always on commission, aggressive salespersons will endow their products with near omnipotence. Software houses and independent programmers are often as inaccurate about their products and capabilities. Accordingly, one must be extremely careful when selecting a piece of hardware or software.

While the situation is now changing, by and large today's computers and computer software are not well human-engineered primarily because they are usually developed by engineers and not users. Over the years this has contributed to poor "man-machine relations" which, in turn, has soured many enthusiastic users. Problem-solvers who are eager to compute should thus take great care to match the hardware and software to their own experience and preferences.

Finally, too many problem-solvers believe that computer software can replace skill, training, and intelligence. Such views are of course false and very dangerous. Regardless of how well designed and instructive a program may be, it can never replace an understanding of what is unfolding on the terminal screen. At the same time, computing can well extend and supplement one's knowledge and experience in ways which can exceed the help and advice of numerous human assistants.

The disadvantages of computer-based problem-solving are listed below:

♦ Hardware and Software Incompatibility

♦ Poor Service

♦ Good Versus Great Programmers

♦ Vendor Oversell

♦ Poor "Man-Machine Relations"

SUMMARY

The process of analytical problem-solving has been changed forever by the revolution in information processing. Today it is possible to compute analytically any statistic interactively and at little cost (relative to just ten years ago). Countless programs are available from the U.S. government, commercial software vendors, and in-house software departments. Mailing lists, distribution lists, schedules, Gantt charts, CPM charts, data inventories, talent rosters, interview data, and even telephone numbers can be stored effortlessly on a computer tape or disk and accessed just as easily. But there are problems with computer-based problem-solving, not the least of which include system incompatibility, poor service, vendor oversell, and less than human-engineered interfaces. A *careful* problem-solver can nevertheless easily configure a cost-effective computer-based problem-solving system.

BIBLIOGRAPHIC ESSAY

The literature on computer science, information systems, and the interface between computers and analytical problem-solving is exploding. Charles J. Sippl and Roger J. Sippl's *Computer Dictionary and Handbook* (Indianapolis: Howard W. Sams, 1980), and Myles E. Walsh's *Understanding Computers: What Managers and Users Need to Know* (New York: Wiley-Interscience, 1981) are excellent beginning/ reference texts. Even more basic are Karen Billings and David Moursand's *Are You Computer Literate* (Portland: Dilithium Press, 1979), *Computer Consciousness: Surviving the Automated 80s* by H. Dominic Covvey and Neil Harding McAllister (Reading, MA: Addison-Wesley, 1980), and Paul M. Chirlian's *Understanding Computers* (Portland: Dilithium Press, 1978). If you are considering purchasing a micro- or mini-computer system, take a look at Raymond P. Capece's edited *Personal Computing: Hardware and Software Basics* (New York: McGraw-Hill, 1979); *How to Buy and Use Minicomputers and Microcomputers* (Indianapolis: Howard W. Sams, 1976) by William Barden, Jr. and Michael Waite; and Michael Pardee's *Your Own Computer* (Indianapolis: Howard W. Sams, 1977). On a slightly higher level are Waite and Pardee's *Microcomputer Primer* (Indianapolis: Howard W. Sams, 1980), and Robert Allen Bonelli's *The Executive's Handbook to Minicomputers* (Princeton, N.J.: Petrocelli Books, 1978). If you are immersed in in-house or service bureau time-sharing, see Timothy P. Haidinger and Dana R. Richardson's *A Manager's Guide to Computer Timesharing* (New York: Wiley-Interscience, 1975). If you are curious about the thousands of computer systems and data bases maintained by the federal government, see *Federal Information Sources and Systems*, a mammoth directory issued by the U.S. Comptroller General (Washington, D.C.: U.S. Government Printing Office, PAD–80–50), and if you are interested in computer programs developed at the taxpayers' expense, contact the many federal research offices and agencies directly, such as the Office of Naval Research, the Defense Advanced Research Projects Agency, the Army Research Institute for the Social and Behavioral Sciences, the National Institutes of Health, and the National Science Foundation, among many, many other offices and agencies. The Lockheed Dialog system discussed in chapter 2 can be very helpful in the search for federally funded computer programs via access to the National Technical Information Service (NTIS), Defense Documentation Center (DDC), and Smithsonian Science Information Exchange (SSIE) data bases. Information about the capabilities of SPSS can be found in Norman H. Nie, C. Hadlai Hull, Jean G. Jenkins, Karin Strinbrenner, and Dale H. Bent's *SPSS* (New York: McGraw-Hill, 1975). For some advice about how to deal with computing problems, see Josh Martin's "Coping with Vendor Failings" (*Computer Decisions*, May 1981, pp. 131–144, 182–192).

12

Summary and Conclusions

IT IS DIFFICULT to summarize the above eleven chapters easily. A great deal of material has been presented in a relatively few number of pages. Yet, it is hoped a number of specific problem-solving principles, strategies, and tactics have evolved.

At the highest—almost philosophical—level, problem-solvers should incessantly remain aware that effective and complete problem-solving is *process oriented*. Comprised of a set of interrelated steps, the problem-solving process is analogous to what is known in computer science as "throughput."

Hovering within and around the process is a set of necessary and sufficient conditions of effective problem-solving. Some of these include the continual awareness of the *tools of problem-solving*:

- ♦ Talent
- ♦ Data
- ♦ Methods
- ♦ Approaches
- ♦ Time
- ♦ Support

But without *organization* tools go unused or—worse—misused. Problem-solvers must thus continually conduct *requirements analyses*, *identify problems* accurately, engage in realistic *constraint analyses*, carefully *structure problems* before attempting to solve them, and then efficiently *plan* and *manage* the problem-solving project.

Organized problem-solving generally directs itself toward the following kinds of problems:

- Descriptive Problems
- Explanatory Problems
- Predictive Problems
- Prescriptive Problems
- Evaluative Problems
- Documentation Problems
- "Defense" Problems

Descriptive problems can be tackled with the aid of *statistical operations* geared to profile empirically some event, condition, or object. Such operations include the use of descriptive or summary statistics which help to characterize observed phenomena. But one can also describe in *narrative* form. Narratives subjected to special scrutiny can be composed via *content analysis*, and opinions, judgments, and even ideas can be polled through *survey techniques*. Finally, *typologies, taxonomies*, and *classificatory schemes* can be used to present descriptive findings in ways which highlight the similarities and differences among the described.

Explanatory problems can be addressed systematically through the statistical techniques of *association, correlation*, and/or *regression*. All of these techniques require *model or framework construction* to some degree, and all require data, skill, time, patience, and computers.

Predictive problems are frequently tackled by "experts" using subjective methods, such as *Delphi, cross-impact*, and the use of *Bayes' theorem of conditional probabilities*. But they can also be solved via objective methods like *multiple regression, causal modeling*, and *econometrics*. All of these methods require data and expertise, and can be dramatically improved by computer support (indeed, the objective methods must be computer-based).

Prescriptive problems include those which require that decisions be made based upon a rational process of goal optimization. Subjective techniques, like those based upon *Bayesian (and other) decision analytic techniques* are especially useful, as are more *empirical option selection techniques*.

Evaluative problems break-down into two broad categories: process and entity evaluation. *Process evaluative analytical problems* involve assessing the behavior of process inputs, workings, and outputs. *Entity evaluative problems* generally concentrate upon objects, ends, outputs, and overall performance. Both kinds of problems are addressable via *subjective* and *objective* methodologies. *Multi-attribute utility methods* are particularly useful subjective methods (especially in their computerized forms). *Empirical utility analysis*, provided data and reliable evaluative measures can be obtained, is also a useful objective method. Finally, *resource allocation*, a special evaluative problem, is addressable via *subjective cost-benefit* and *objective linear programming* methodologies.

Documentation problems always accompany the problem-solving process. *Written documentation*, in the form of reports and memoranda, are by far the most common form. Written reports and memoranda should be concise, clear, and free of unneccessary technical jargon. They should also be preceded by crisp overviews or executive summaries. *Verbal presentations* of documented findings should speak closely to the written record and be carefully staged because of potential unanticipated attitude changes on the part of problem-generators. *Documentation distribution* should be made according to established procedure, problem-solver vested interests, and in the interests of pure communication. *Unconventional documentation* can be accomplished via videotapes, videodiscs, tape recordings, 35mm slides, and overhead viewgraphs.

Finally, the problem-solving process frequently places the problem-solver in a *defensive posture* where he or she must actually convince, persuade, and/or cajole solution-consumers about the validity—and sometimes even relevance—of their work. Consequently, problem-solvers must become skilled in the art and science of *negotiation*, *persuasion*, and *structured briefings*. They must also remain aware of the bureaucratic environment in which they function.

The entire problem-solving process can be enhanced with the aid of computers. In particular, since computers are now small, relatively inexpensive, and pre-programmed, it is now possible to personalize the computer-based problem-solving process. Specifically, *computers can routinize* many problem-solving requirements, they can *document* the problem-solving process automatically, they can *teach* and *instruct*, they can assist with the *distribution* of findings, they can *alleviate many support burdens*, and they can facilitate *creative problem-solving* through the development of *hybrid computer-based methodologies*. Problem-solvers can also benefit from the many, many *software systems* which are available at modest cost and which can help solve many kinds of problems. On the negative side, however, *computer software is frequently incompatible*, as is hardware. Computers are often *serviced poorly* and *great programmeers are very hard to find*. *Vendor oversell* is also a big problem, and many software systems are so *poorly human-engineered* that users become easily and sometimes permanently frustrated.

Good problem-solvers are those who work at it. Many of the ideas and suggestions presented in this handbook presume a substantial amount of effort on the part of the reader. The bibliographic essays which follow the sections are filled with books, articles, and reports which point the reader in the right direction, but they must be acquired and studied. In large measure, then, this handbook in intended to introduce some new techniques to analytical problem-solvers. The real work lies ahead.

It is also important to note once again that problem-solving is a dynamic unpredictable process. Just as new methods and techniques evolve so too do the organizational/administrative rules of the game change frequently. Problem-solving today is as much a "social" process as it is an analytical one. No longer can problem-solvers perceive themselves or actually behave akin to abstract scientists unconcerned or uninvolved with the problem-solving origin or purpose.

Finally, if analytical problem-solving is to be productive and enduring, problem-solvers must incessantly sharpen their skills. I have tried to introduce and describe a whole host of tools, but tomorrow there will be new tools and new problems. Unless we continually study and learn, tomorrow's problems may very well overtake us.

Glossary

ANALOGY. A powerful tool for problem structuring involving the description and application of past problem-solving experiences for present problem-solving. Any method or technique which structures the past for present or future benefit.

APPROACHES. Aggregated criteria for selecting the questions and data to be brought to bear to address a specific problem.

ARGUMENTATION. The process of refutation during the communication and defense of analytical solutions.

BAR CHART. A graphical representation of frequencies displayed as rectangles on a graph.

BATCH COMPUTING. Computer-based problem-solving via the submission of analytical "jobs" for subsequent processing.

BAYESIAN ANALYSIS. The application of information processing techniques and methods based upon Bayes' theorem of conditional probabilities.

BIVARIATE ANALYSIS. The analysis of two variables to determine how they associate, interrelate, and/or co-vary.

BRIEFINGS. Formal structured verbal presentations of analytical research findings usually supported by audiovisual aids.

"BUREAUCRATIC POLITICS." The politics connected with maneuvering through environments defined according to formal and informal rules of behavior frequently inhibited by role playing and the skillful manipulation of the rules.

CAUSAL MODEL. A representation of a set of interrelated variables which directly and indirectly impact upon a dependent variable. When mathematically defined, a causal model is often described as an econometric model.

CHI SQUARE (X^2). A statistical test for determining whether or not (and to what degree) an observed observation could be the result of chance. A .95 chi square would indicate that there was only a 5% chance that the observations had occurred by chance.

CLASSIFICATORY SCHEMA. Lists of variables organized according to a set of characteristics which highlight the similarities and differences among the variables.

COMPARATIVE METHODS. Those methods which focus upon the similarities and differences among the phenomena under investigation.

COMPUTER-BASED PROBLEM-SOLVING. Problem-solving via the application of analytical computer software either interactively or in batch.

COMPUTERIZED INFORMATION BANKS. Information banks, like the *New York Times* Information Bank and the Lockheed Dialog System, which satisfy on-demand requests via access through remote computer terminals.

CONSTRAINT ANALYSIS. The realistic examination of all of the problem-solving constraints which will inhibit the problem-solving process, including the lack of expertise, data, methodological experience, analytical approaches, time, or support.

CONTINGENCY TABLES. Simple data arrays in rows and columns.

COORDINATE GRAPH. A four quadrant scatter diagram for displaying the values of cases according to the high and low values of two variables.

CORRELATION. A statistical procedure for measuring the relationship between two or more variables.

COST-BENEFIT ANALYSIS. Resource allocation and evaluation based upon subjective and objective cost and benefit assessments.

CPM CHART. A *critical path method* to identify, interrelate, and time-estimate project tasks. A management tool for describing and projecting project progress.

CROSS-IMPACT METHODS. Prediction and forecasting methods which recognize and define the co-impact of events. Yield probabilities of events based upon probabilities of other events.

DATA AND INFORMATION. Subjective and objective opinions and facts used to describe, explain, predict, prescribe, and evaluate.

DATA RELIABILITY. The confidence one has in a given objective or subjective data set, given its known strengths and weaknesses.

DATA SELECTOR. A device for the evaluation and selection of data based upon multiple criteria, including cost, reliability, availability, and format.

DECISION ANALYSIS. The application of a formal quantitative method for decomposing decision situations according to the costs, benefits, and likelihoods connected with various decision alternatives.

DECISION MODELS. Descriptive, explanatory, prescriptive, predictive, or evaluative representations of the relationships among decision-making procedures and decision-makers.

DECISION TREE. Graphic representation of decision options, costs, and benefits, and the probabilities of key uncertainties permitting the evaluation of decision alternatives.

DEDUCTIVE METHODS. Those methods which involve the extraction of knowledge from existing analytical premises.

DEFENSE. The process by which analytical solutions are explained, communicated, and defended usually via briefings, argumentation, and negotiation.

DELPHI METHODS. Forecasting procedures whereby experts express formal judgments and opinions about the likelihood of future events and/or conditions anonymously and in multiple rounds in response to the feedback gained from the prior round.

DEPENDENT VARIABLE. The object or target of descriptive, explanatory, and predictive analyses. Defined, described, explained, and predicted according to measurable changes in the independent variable(s).

DESCRIPTION. The process by which events and conditions are profiled in order to determine similarities, differences, ranges, variations, and interrelationships.

"DISCIPLINED" APPROACHES. Those problem-solving approaches which are categorizable according to the academic disciplines from which they borrow, including economic, psychological, and historical approaches.

DOCUMENTATION. Reports, memoranda, presentations, videotape, videodiscs, tape recordings, slides, viewgraphs, and all other written or audiovisual means by which analytical results are described.

DYNAMIC PROGRAMMING. A mathematical technique for making sequential allocation decisions.

ECONOMETRIC MODELS. Complex representations of phenomena via the development of multiple interrelated regression equations. Mathematically defined causal models.

EMPIRICAL DATA. Data and information which is extracted from empirical observations.

ENTITY EVALUATION. The evaluation of systems, people, and other "static" phenomena which can be compared via the assessment of explicit, mutually exclusive criteria; distinct from the evaluation of processes.

EPISTEMOLOGY. The sub-field of philosophy which focuses upon the origin, nature, methods, and limits of knowledge.

EVAL. A microcomputer program which permits the evaluation of entities through the decomposition of evaluative criteria and scoring against the criteria. (Also useful for the evaluation of decision options.)

EVALUABILITY ASSESSMENT. The process by which it is determined whether or not a process or entity can be meaningfully evaluated.

EVALUATION. The process by which entities and processes are evaluated against sets of explicit evaluative criteria.

"EXPERT" JUDGMENTS. Judgments or opinions elicited from recognized experts and then brought to bear upon an analytical problem. On the opposite end of the epistemological continuum from quantitative-empirical data or information.

EXPLANATION. The process by which events and conditions, often expressed as variables, are linked to one another in measurable relationships whereby the changes in one set of variables can be related to changes in another set of variables.

EXTRAPOLATIVE FORECASTING METHODS. Those methods which rely upon the persistence of data over time, the projection of trends, simulations, scenarios, moving averages, and exponential smoothing in order to predict or forecast events and/or conditions.

FAULT TREES. Graphical displays of processes, entities, and/or systems of decomposed elements and sub-elements then used as a framework for pinpointing problems.

FRAMEWORKS. Devices which identify, arrange, and interrelate variables in a way which permits the development of analytical models and testable hypotheses.

FREQUENCY DISTRIBUTION. The presentation of data according to a specific variable in a graph, table, or chart.

FUNCTIONAL APPROACHES. Those problem-solving approaches which are categorizable according to the functions they seek to describe, explain, predict, forecast, prescribe, or evaluate, such as legal approaches, communications approaches, and systems approaches.

GANTT CHART. A management tool for identifying and time-estimating project tasks according to a specific time schedule.

GROUP DECISION-MAKING. The process by which more than one individual solves a decision problem, usually characterized by conflicting images and perceptions, role playing, and "bureaucratic politics."

HIERARCHICAL INFERENCE STRUCTURING. A subjective forecasting technique which requires the identification and hierarchical organization of the activities, indicators, and data likely to impact probabilistically upon a set of mutually exclusive hypotheses.

HYPOTHESIS. An "if . . . then" statement frequently used to structure problems, brainstorm, and determine how variables interrelate statistically.

INDEPENDENT VARIABLE. A variable hypothesized as influential upon a dependent variable. When tested and found to have measurable impact upon a dependent variable, it can be offered as a descriptive, explanatory, or predictive variable.

INDUCTIVE METHODS. Those methods which involve the extraction of knowledge from perceptions of reality.

INTERACTIVE COMPUTING. Immediate, on-line problem-solving via computer programs designed to respond directly to their users.

INTERVAL LEVEL DATA. Data having equal intervals such as temperatures and speed.

LINEAR PROGRAMMING. A mathematical method for allocating resources given known constraints.

LINEAR RELATIONSHIPS. Straight line relationships without exponents, where the value of the dependent variable (Y) is predictably and linearly related to the value of the independent variable (X).

MEASURES OF CENTRAL TENDENCY. Several statistics which summarize "center" data values, including the mean, median, and mode.

MEASURES OF VARIABILITY. Several statistics which summarize the variability of data around its "middle" value, including the range and standard deviation.

METHODS. The means by which data and information are organized and manipulated, in conjunction with analytical approaches in order to "solve" analytical problems.

MILESTONE CHART. A management tool for identifying project tasks and when they will be completed.

MINI-DELPHI METHODS. Abbreviated forecasting procedures for conducting face-to-face Delphi exercises. Implemented when time and money are in short supply.

MODELS. Representations of reality described graphically or mathematically, but always incompletely.

MULTI-ATTRIBUTE UTILITY ANALYSIS. Analysis which permits the evaluation of decision options and entities according to multidimensional definition of "value" or "worth," which always involves the identification of multiple evaluative criteria.

MULTIPLE CORRELATION AND REGRESSION. A statistical technique which permits the analysis of more than two independent variables vis-a-vis a dependent variable.

MULTIVARIATE ANALYSIS. The analysis of more than two variables to describe, explain, or predict phenomena.

NEGOTIATION. The process of compromise during the communication and defense of analytical solutions.

NOMINAL LEVEL DATA. Data categorizable only by name, such as days of the week and months of the year.

ORDINAL LEVEL DATA. Measurable data without equal intervals, such as student grades where the 500th student is by no means 4 times the worker the 125th student is.

PREDICTION AND FORECASTING. The process by which future events and/or conditions are identified and assessed.

PREDICTION AND FORECASTING GOALS. Short-, medium-, and long-range, negative and positive, objective and normative predictive-forecasting goals which, together with objects, define the parameters of the predictive-forecasting problem.

PREDICTION AND FORECASTING OBJECTS. Events or conditions which, along with the identification of goals, define the parameters of the predictive-forecasting problem.

PRESCRIPTION. The selection from competing alternatives of a single option. Recommendations made on the basis of analytical steps taken to resolve uncertainty in a decision situation.

PROBABILITY DIAGRAMS. Graphic representations of the events and/or conditions likely to affect the probability of a target event or condition. Yield quantitative probabilities from calculation of "path" probabilities.

PROBLEM CERTIFICATION MEMORANDUM. A formal memorandum, prepared by the problem-solver and signed by the problem-generator, which describes and certifies the problem to be tackled.

PROBLEM SOLVING CHECKLIST. A formal or informal device for determining whether or not the tools of problem-solving are adequate and available. Always used *before* problem-solving begins.

PROBLEM-SOLVING DELEGATION. The process of assigning appropriate problem-solving roles to available talent recognizing each individual's strengths and weaknesses.

PROBLEM-SOLVING ORGANIZATION. The aggregate process comprised of requirements analyses, problem identification, problem structuring, constraint analyses, and project management.

PROBLEM-SOLVING PROCESS. The process of tool assessment, organization, documentation, and defense, and the selection and implementation of descriptive, explanatory, predictive, prescriptive, and evaluative analytical methodologies—all in an effort to solve a specific analytical problem.

PROBLEM-SOLVING TOOLS. Problem-solving talent, data and information, methods, approaches, time, and support.

PROBLEM STRUCTURING. All activity designed to profile the essence of a problem-solving situation frequently involving the use of analogy, analytical frameworks, models, and hypothesis formation.

PROCESS EVALUATION. The evaluation of on-going, active processes via a set of criteria or explicit process goals; distinct from the evaluation of entities.

PRODUCT MOMENT CORRELATION COEFFICIENTS. The statistic which measures the strength of the relationship between interval level variables. The squared correlation coefficient (r^2) is the coefficient of determination which signifies the variance of one variable which is explained by the variance in the other.

PROJECT MANAGEMENT. The tasks and sub-tasks connected with the organization, implementation, scheduling, and monitoring of analytical projects.

QUALITATIVE METHODS. Those methods which rely primarily upon the collection and manipulation of subjective or expert-generated data.

QUANTITATIVE METHODS. Those methods which rely primarily upon the collection and manipulation of quantitative-empirical, or objective, data.

QUESTIONNAIRE DESIGN. The complex and exacting process by which questions are structured, arranged, and presented orally or on paper in order to conduct requirements analyses and surveys.

RAM. A computer-based *r*esource *a*llocation *m*odeling system for allocating scarce resources according to subjective cost-benefit assessments.

RANK-ORDER DISPLAYS. A graphical display of variables ranked from highest to lowest and interconnected according to how they interrelate.

REGRESSION. A statistical technique for measuring and defining the relationship between two or more variables in predictive terms.

REPORT DISTRIBUTION. The strategy by which analytical reports and memoranda are distributed throughout an organization designed to maximize impact and minimize bureaucratic fallout.

REPRESENTATIVE SAMPLES. Samples which in fact measure what they purport to measure. Representative samples are the result of skillfully implemented sampling procedures and questionnaires.

REQUIREMENTS ANALYSIS. The application of a variety of techniques for determining the characteristics of the problem to be tackled. The techniques include the use of questionnaires, critical incident profiling, and fault trees.

RESOURCE ALLOCATION. The process by which limited resources are allocated across specific functions optimally against a set of priorities.

SCATTER PLOTS. A graphic representation of the frequencies on a standard graph displayed by dots within the vertical and horizontal axes.

SPEARMAN'S RHO. An ordinal level statistical test for determining the extent of the relationship between two variables ranging from -1 to $+1$.

STANDARD DEVIATION. The meausure of dispersion around the mean (or average) value of a set of frequency data points which measures just how spread out and consistent the data set is.

STATISTICAL SIGNIFICANCE. The results of significance tests to determine the likelihood of empirical observations occurring by chance. Test results below .95 mean that there is less than enough confidence to declare the observations statistically significant. Some often used significance tests include Chi Square (X^2), F tests, Fisher exact tests, and D tests.

SPURIOUS RELATIONSHIPS. Relationships which may be highly associated but completely unrelated causally.

SUBJECTIVE DATA. Data and information which is elicited from experts.

SUPPORT. Human, mechanical, and electronic problem-solving apparati necessary for efficient and successful problem-solving.

TALENT. Problem-solving expertise comprised of skill, experience, attitude, education, and training.

TALENT ROSTERING. The process of maintaining lists of experts across as many fields as necessary to satisfy problem-solving requirements.

TALENT SELECTOR. A device for the evaluation and selection of problem-solving based upon multiple criteria, including skill, education, experience, cost, availability, and attitude.

TAXONOMIES. Classificatory devices for highlighting the similarities and differences among phenomena.

TIME. A problem-solving tool whose effect can be maximized by the elimination of time-wasting activity and development of systematic time-scheduling procedures.

TIME PLANNING. The allocation of time resources; systematic time scheduling.

TIME WASTERS. All activity, such as unnecessarily long phone conversations, local and overnight travel, and meetings which do not contribute directly or even indirectly to problem-solving.

TYPOLOGIES. Formal devices which classify phenomena according to characteristics which are exclusive to the type. Knowledge of the type in a typology permits the prediction of specific characteristics and vice versa.

UNCONVENTIONAL DOCUMENTATION. The use of videotape, videodiscs, slides, viewgraphs, tape recordings, and other audiovisual aids and devices to report on an analytical project.

UNIVARIATE ANALYSIS. The analysis of a single variable to determine how it deviates within itself.

YULE'S Q. A statistical test which measures the degree and direction of bivariate (two variable) associations, ranging from -1 to +1.

Index